For Thomas Abraham, the elephant catcher

THE ELEPHANT CATCHERS

Subroto Bagchi co-founded Mindtree Ltd, one of India's first software services start-ups, in 1999. Author of the bestsellers *The High-Performance Entrepreneur, Go Kiss the World, The Professional, MBA at 16* and *The Professional Companion*, Bagchi was acclaimed as India's No. 1 bestselling business books' author. His works have been translated into several languages, including Hindi, Marathi, Malayalam, Tamil, Kannada, Korean and Chinese.

Bagchi now works full-time as Chairman of the Odisha Skill Development Authority.

Praise for *The Elephant Catchers*

'Practical advice on real issues... Bagchi uses his years of on-the-ground learning and experience to explore [...] what organizations and their people need to do to climb to the next level and beyond.'

– *The Hindu*

'[Bagchi] knows how to tell a good story...'

– *Business Standard*

'Bagchi explores...concepts with simple analogies drawn from his own growth as an entrepreneur. Embellished with anecdotes and stories, [*The Elephant Catchers*] makes for an easy read.'

– *Business Line*

'Bagchi's credit lies in his efforts to humanize business... [H]e has always managed to take note of the human at the core...a rare trait in businessmen anywhere!'

– *Business India*

'When it is about management mantras, [Bagchi] is the go-to guru.'

– *Bangalore Mirror*

'A must-read for anyone in business.'

– *Deccan Herald*

'[Bagchi] has mastered the art of blending almost a perfect brew of business reality, high-performance imperative with integrity and soft spirituality.'

– *Management Next*

SUBROTO BAGCHI

THE ELEPHANT CATCHERS

KEY LESSONS FOR BREAKTHROUGH GROWTH

hachette INDIA

First published in 2013 by Hachette India
(Registered name: Hachette Book Publishing India Pvt. Ltd)
An Hachette UK company
www.hachetteindia.com

This revised and expanded edition published in paperback in 2017

SRD

Hardback edition ISBN 978-93-5009-583-6
Paperback edition ISBN 978-93-5195-000-4
Ebook edition ISBN 978-93-5009-672-7

Hachette Book Publishing India Pvt. Ltd
4th & 5th Floors, Corporate Centre,
Plot No. 94, Sector 44, Gurugram - 122003, India

Typeset in Guardi Lt Std 10/16.8
by Inosoft Systems, Noida

Printed and bound in India by
Manipal Technologies Limited, Manipal

MIX
Paper from responsible sources
FSC™ C043100

CONTENTS

Introduction **ix**

PART I THE IDEA OF SCALE

Lessons from a Swami **3**

Murder in New York **11**

A Bamboo Bridge to Cross the Ocean **21**

The Elephant Catchers **29**

PART II SCALING YOUR BUSINESS

The Cat and Dog Differential **41**

Of Hunters, Farmers, Grizzlies and Skunks **51**

Marriages of Convenience **61**

The M&A Myths **71**

Value, Valuation & the Roll-Up Kids **81**

PART III SCALING YOUR INTELLECT

The Wise Men around the Table **93**

When the Shepherd Needs Help **101**

PART IV SCALING YOUR REPUTATION

A Brand New You 113
The Fourth Estate 123
The Force of Good 131

PART V SCALING YOUR PEOPLE

Hire Right, Fire Right 143
Are you Buoyant? 157
The Fashion-Designer Nun 165
Square Pegs and Round Holes 177
Gardening Tales 187
When Brahma Fails 197

PART VI SCALING AGAINST ADVERSITY

Rites of Passage 209
Bolts from the Blue 217

Acknowledgements 231

AFTERWORD NEW STORIES, FURTHER LESSONS

Amazing Stories of Scale 235
The Challenges to Scaling Up 246
The Six Elements of Scaling Up 254

INTRODUCTION

IN 2006, MY BOOK *The High-Performance Entrepreneur* broke new ground as a must-read for would-be entrepreneurs. It became immensely popular among an entire generation of young Indians who dreamt beyond getting a job, about building businesses and creating jobs for others. The book was based on my experiences of failure at starting a company when I was 28 and then successfully co-founding Mindtree when I was 42. Through these two experiences and my observations of many great entrepreneurs, the book stated my belief that start-ups must be designed for high performance and that this is not impossible to achieve.

In the intervening years, a lot has changed in my life as a professional and an entrepreneur. In 2007, Mindtree got its public listing. Listing a company at the stock exchange is the ultimate dream of every start-up. But taking a company to that stage brings with it the obligation of growth. Quite naturally, after 2007, all our endeavours and transformative experiences have had a lot to do with the challenge of scaling.

In some ways, starting something is easier than scaling it. That is why people and their businesses hit the proverbial glass ceiling despite a successful start. *The Elephant Catchers* synthesizes my learning of the last few years and contains a collection of hard-earned lessons on a spectrum of issues around the core idea of scaling an organization and its people.

The book is arranged in six sections. In Part I, I present the need to build comfort with the idea of scale and the essentials that go with it. Part II is about getting the large deals that will help scale your business and the kind of people you must employ to get them, about staying away from certain customer engagements and business models that could prevent growth, and about mergers and acquisitions (M&As) that invariably engage every organization at some stage or the other. In Part III, the conversation shifts to the idea that sustaining an enterprise is a game of intellect. The capacity to get to the next level often depends on a leader's ability to augment organizational intellect by tapping into external expertise. I have given a few pointers here on how it can be done most effectively. Part IV deals with the reputation of an organization. Reputation is a form of capital and growing it right, beyond just good public relations, is something that organizations often overlook. In Part V, the focus is on the importance of scaling people at every level of the organization. The modern enterprise is all about people, be it the management and leaders, or the employees. It addresses the need for intelligent recruitment; the traps that leaders fall into, causing the organization to stall; and issues of succession and nurturing the next generation of leaders. Part VI tells you about the final frontier, where the leader must scale his own 'self'. We all know that behind every organization there is the leader who sets it on its path. A time comes when the leader himself is required to pass tests that come in his way in the form of certain rites of passage and bolts from the blue. The response of the leader, sometimes deeply personal, defines the destiny of the organization.

The core idea of scale and its associated attributes and challenges are not unique to for-profit businesses. These are equally applicable to any institution and, I can even say, every individual. I hope that in this book you will be able to get some insight about your own organization and yourself. For that, I ask you to bear with me when you see terms like 'leader', 'founder', 'entrepreneur', 'manager' or 'management'. I have used these words interchangeably. Similarly, when you come across the words 'start-up', 'company', 'institution' or 'organization', please interpret it as a placeholder for a larger idea. All of them will fit into two classifications: those that scale and those that don't. The broad considerations why some do and some don't stay the same irrespective of the kind of organization they are.

The original manuscript had a 'she' for every 'he', because that is how it largely is in the modern workplace. But my editor, Poulomi Chatterjee, struck this down in the interest of easy readability. So, wherever you see a 'he', please do not conjure a male image. Instead, think of my editor.

The Elephant Catchers does not pretend to be the complete book on the subject of scale. I am not a management guru; I am a mere practitioner. To that extent my lessons could be imperfect, but they are real. All the experiences I have written about in this book have been lived by me. I would also like to remind my readers that Mindtree is my platform, my high-sea rig, my runway. I take off from it and land on it. References to Mindtree in this book are meant to bring to you real experiences and, through these, to share real lessons. It is not to suggest that Mindtree is the shining example of scale. I always tell my colleagues that we walk in the shadows of giants, and I truly believe that.

Lastly, the purpose of this book is not to glorify scale. It is to tell you how to scale if you want to, need to, and if you must. Some things in life are meant to stay small and life has a way of ensuring everything has its place. I hope you find the book useful as you set out on your own journey to take your life and your enterprise someplace.

PART I

THE IDEA OF SCALE

1

LESSONS FROM A SWAMI

> 'Those who do not embrace the notion of size and cannot enjoy magnitude will always have problems with it.'

SOME YEARS AGO I was invited to give a talk at the Siddaganga Institute of Technology in Tumkur, near Bengaluru. It was set up in 1963 by a religious trust called Sree Siddaganga Mutt, which has been in existence since the fifteenth century CE. The current head of the institution, known reverentially as 'Swamiji', assumed charge of the institution sometime in the 1930s. Today, the trust runs many schools, and engineering and management colleges, that thousands of students attend from all around the country.

After my talk, I was driven to the village where Swamiji, who is now 106 years old, lives. Within the village, surrounded by temples, residences and a few shops, is a large, open space, a giant courtyard. When I arrived there dusk was setting in and it was time for the evening prayers. As our car pulled up at the entrance to the village, I witnessed one of the most spectacular sights I have ever experienced. The courtyard was filling up really fast with boys of all ages pouring in from every direction. Some were running around and some were huddled in groups, but there was great energy and joy on every face. The entire place hummed with their excitement. To my astonishment, I was told that 8,500 boys had gathered there!

The chattering of the children in front of me was like the sound you would hear under the canopy of a large tree when thousands of birds come home, circle their nests, and make joyful noises before settling down. Then, just like the birds suddenly become quiet and become one with the canopy above, the children too stopped scampering around and squatted in the courtyard in neat rows. It was time for them to sing their hymns. The voices, thousands in unison, sang the evening prayers as Swamiji sat in deep meditation beyond the sea of lowered heads.

After singing the hymns, the boys rose and ran towards their hostels with the same childlike abandon with which they had arrived. It was time for them to collect their plates and go to the dining hall where a wholesome but simple meal awaited them. I sat down among them to eat their fare. My host, the principal of the engineering college set up by the Mutt, was seated next to me. He told me that he was a product of this very institution. At one time he too had been like the children we were sitting with. These boys, all from neighbouring villages, had been left in the care of the Mutt by their parents.

Story has it that a long time ago there was a terrible drought in the area. People had nothing to eat, nothing to sustain their families with. In despair, they brought their little ones and left them in Swamiji's care in the hope that the children, at least, would survive the ordeal. Swamiji took them all under his wing; he fed them, looked after their well-being and started schooling them. When the tides turned, the villagers came in hordes to return the favour he had done them, and ever since, every year, they continue to bring him a part of their produce and leave behind some of their progeny to be educated at the Mutt. Swamiji continues to take them all in. They live in frugal quarters, eat regular meals and study as all other children do. The lessons and everyday activities follow quite seamlessly, and even if a child fails in a certain year he is not turned away. The Mutt takes care of them till they pass high school. All of this at no cost to the students. From the time it began, the institute has grown from less than a hundred students to its current size of 8,500.

At the end of this fantastic experience, I was left with many questions. How does Swamiji manage size, I wondered. How is it that his institution has not caved in, while so many start-up companies led by able, astute and committed individuals struggle acutely with growth after their initial success?

In today's world, for most organizations, growth is no longer an option; it is imperative. If you look at it from another perspective, as you were growing up, you could make a few mistakes and you could take your own time learning from them. As an adult, while you are still entitled to make a few mistakes, you neither have the luxury of making them repeatedly nor do you have time on your side. In the same way, there was a time when you could start your business and allow it to grow at a pace that you determined. In today's highly competitive environment, organizations are compelled to shed their baby-fat really fast. The situation has changed drastically from the time an entrepreneur was among a handful of people with a bright idea. Knowledge, and knowledge about that knowledge, was scarce, and you could work on your idea assiduously in a womb-like, secure space until you were ready for the world, with very few chances of someone else beating you to your game. The internet has taken away that security. Whatever your product or service may be, there are a dozen others who are busy manufacturing the very same mousetrap even as you are reading this. It follows that it is no longer enough to just start a business. Sustained growth, growth that is often exponential and not incremental, is essential for success.

Yet, most people are inherently fearful of the idea of growth, some of them for reasons that are perfectly understandable. With growth comes flux, which makes many people insecure. Very few people like to work in a large, impersonal set-up where, they fear, they will lose their identity. They crave the nascent stages of a start-up in which goals, values and enthusiasm were equally shared.

Management theory falls short in giving us a fool-proof formula that can help us balance growth and scale with stability and harmony. Driving back from Sree Siddaganga Mutt that night, I couldn't help reflecting on what I had observed of the Mutt's daily functioning and the leader who made it possible in this context.

To begin with, Swamiji is at peace with size. The idea of scale does not daunt him. Just thinking of all the risks one could run into in trying to manage 8,500 boys between the ages of five and sixteen could have made anyone a nervous wreck. If Swamiji was fundamentally not at peace with the fact that he had the welfare of 8,500 children to think of, there is no way that the place could have existed even for a short while.

Swamiji has no elaborate scheme, no articulated strategy for raising funds to feed and clothe and educate the children. There is no sophisticated computerized information system or even the barest tools without which a modern manager would freeze in his tracks. Despite all that, the Mutt obviously gets what it needs, sometimes in small measures and sometimes large, and has managed itself in the face of difficulties and challenges. In this, Swamiji's most fundamental ally has been his sense of purpose, the purpose of serving the surrounding communities through the education of their children. That purpose is so powerful that it permeates everything; it is the force that binds everyone in the Mutt and creates alignment. It is the purpose that determines Swamiji's power to take growth and scale in his stride without being daunted by the idea and causing the place to fall apart.

Of the 8,500 children I saw, no two boys are similar and no two of them come from the same microcosm. Yet, for decades, children have arrived here, studied and grown up, graduated, and gone their own ways. Over the years, no less than 100,000 boys have passed through the Mutt and gone on to make their own living in this world. As they become part of the ethos, they embrace something very interesting: a high degree of self-regulation. This is a pervasive theme at the Siddaganga Mutt. As remarkable as the sense of orderliness and peace that prevailed in the place was, I was more amazed by the fact that I rarely saw an adult supervising the thousands of children there. They went about their tasks in perfect order and coordination with very little visible supervision. During the evening prayers, when an unexpected downpour occurred, a section of the gathering got up and ran to take shelter. No one had instructed these children to go, or told the others to stay. Then, as the rain stopped as suddenly as it had started, the boys ran back to join the others and the prayers continued as if nothing had happened. A self-regulating operating system was clearly at work. It extended to larger and smaller decisions; decisions that were being taken by the children themselves. And it is common knowledge that a self-regulating system minimizes the need for bureaucracy.

The other astounding thing I noticed about the Mutt was its simplicity. Simplicity is a powerful tool in any human effort. A simple communication is more powerful than a complex one. A simple organization is easier to work for than a complex one. A simple product design lends itself better to manufacturing and maintenance than a complicated one. Yet, simplicity is a discipline that requires cultivation over years and can be achieved only through conscious effort. When I was in conversation with Swamiji before dinner, the thing that struck me most was his personal simplicity. He spoke little but spoke clearly. He enquired if I understood Kannada, his mother tongue. When I said I didn't, he immediately switched to English. He spoke to me about things I was familiar with. He talked to me about the software industry boom and the Indian economy, among other things. It was clear that the simplicity that he embodied permeated the organizational structure, the systems, processes and methodologies that governed every activity in the Mutt.

It also struck me that accessibility plays an important part in maintaining the balance and security that is essential in keeping the place together. In the Mutt, anyone can ask for an audience with Swamiji. Sometimes it includes some of the youngest ones who demand his mediation to resolve a fight!

There are innumerable lessons we can learn from Swamiji. He has, after all, managed to create a balanced eco-system that allows size and speed to take their natural course while ensuring that the sense of identity that smallness gives is retained. Above everything else, behind the remarkable story of the Siddaganga Mutt is one man's comfort with the idea of scale. Those who do not embrace the notion of size and cannot enjoy magnitude will always have problems with it. Swamiji does not see growth as a nuisance. He sees it as an ally, as a welcome way to expand capacity and, from there on, to make a difference.

2

MURDER IN NEW YORK

> ‘If you are not ambitious enough to scale, and scale big, you will not need to engage with the term ‘strategy’.’

AT SREE SIDDAGANGA MUTT, you can engage anyone in a conversation on the uplifting idea of ‘purpose’, but consider for a moment having a conversation with the people there on ‘strategy’. However important it may sound, the thought that the place should have a strategy, that it should make provisions for managed growth and de-risking odds, makes for incongruous dialogue. Thank you, but the Siddaganga Mutt does not need a strategy.

That enviable option is not available to people charged with running a for-profit and in some cases even a not-for-profit organization today. Swamiji is in a minority. For you and me, strategy will prove to be the critical difference between helping our organizations sprout and getting them to scale. As with the earliest stages of setting up an organization, the absence of strategy at this critical juncture may lead to an organization's downfall even if its sense of purpose is strong.

I have sat through countless 'strategy' sessions in and outside of Mindtree and found that, quite often, people who are discussing strategy do not really understand its true nature. Strategy and scale go hand in hand. You don't need to think of strategy if incremental growth makes you happy. On the other hand, if you are seized with the ambition of making a big difference, you need a strategy. And you need to understand its true import.

Most professionally run organizations reduce the actual act of strategizing to a formal annual, predictably named 'strategy session', usually held closer to the beginning of the fiscal year to come. Leaders and managers go into a huddle, sub-groups are formed, there are brain-storming sessions, arguments over data and trends, and then some competition analysis is done. The bosses listen to group presentations, devour PowerPoint slides and then go on to do what they have already settled on in their minds. Most people ideating at such annual corporate strategy retreats do not want to fail. To them failure is scary. So they talk about a growth of 10, 15 or 20 per cent over the previous year, they talk about introducing marginal changes in their products and services, they agree to small investments and ask for incremental returns. These people discuss a plan that will extend the lifespan of the group by just about another season. Their stakes are low. This in itself is an indication that ideas of growth, scale and expansion are not involved in their scheme of things, that there is no need for thought that can truly qualify as 'strategic'. If you are not ambitious enough to scale, and scale big, you will not need to engage with the term 'strategy'.

■

Over time, I have come to realize that there is a set of strategy traps leaders routinely fall prey to.

A group that is battling with ways to achieve only incremental growth is not really discussing strategy. It is merely dribbling with a plan to extrapolate from the present. It is looking at a low-risk approach that will yield small upsides.

Similarly, if a group comes up with a plan that does not involve visible personal and organizational displacement, it remains just that – a plan. It is not strategy.

A group may experience an 'aha' moment when it identifies the link between a problem and its solution, but here too it is not being strategic at all. It is not asking enough questions; it is not seeing the big picture; it is not making an intuitive bet.

A strategy that stems from the left brain, arises entirely from data and is based on rational thinking will lack emotional appeal and can never be effectively executed. Great strategy, on the other hand, must have an emotive appeal. Without this, a strategy will not be memorable, and people do not follow what they cannot remember.

Most often, a group in search of the Holy Grail overlooks solutions and strategies that are close at hand, possibly lying under-cultivated or underserved.

Great strategy is not about a pie chart sliced and diced to infinity, then multiplied with a radar graph and divided to death by a 3D histogram. Great strategy is simplicity that even the doorman can understand.

Let's take a look at a few of these factors more closely.

In March 2000, Infosys, India's bellwether IT services company, had 5,389 employees. At this time its leaders decided that Infosys must embrace the idea of scale to become a noticeable, global player in five years' time. They imagined the world of the future, the 'flat world', as Infosys's co-founder Nandan Nilekani famously coined, and determined that to be globally relevant the most important thing they needed to do was to grow significantly in size. Consequently, Infosys grew from 5,389 employees in 2000 to 15,876 in 2003 and 1,30,820 by February 2011. If this rate of growth had come about without conscious strategic thinking and the proper socializing of it with all stakeholders, Infosys would have collapsed. They did not go about randomly hiring people; they thought thoroughly about every aspect – from entry-level training to leadership development, from efficient systems and processes to rewards and recognition, from choice of customers to business models – keeping the theme of rapid growth central.

When teams meet to brainstorm at a strategy retreat, they invariably look to solve an existing problem. In the process, while trying to resolve an issue or seeking a breakthrough, they match a conventional problem with a conventional solution, instead of looking and thinking deep into the issue for a more effective, if radical, solution. If salespeople aren't selling enough, change the commission structure, they will say. If attrition is high, raise salaries and offer a substantial bonus at the time of joining. If customers are going away, pursue them and plead them to stay. And, if you are the mayor of a crime-infested mega-city with a high murder rate, give the homicide officers greater power and go after the perpetrators with a vengeance.

Unless, of course, you are Rudy Giuliani, two-time mayor of New York City. I lived close to New York City during Giuliani's second tenure as mayor and have seen how unsafe the city used to be under previous administrations. When Giuliani took office in 1994, New York City had the dubious distinction of being the murder capital of the world, with more than 2,000 murders reported in a year. Giuliani actioned the police to make the city safe. In doing so, he asked them to go after petty crime and get the panhandlers off the street. Apart from being a nuisance to motorists and pedestrians, the panhandlers were also the last mile in the drug business and, according to one theory, many of the city's killings were drug-related. When the police got to them and broke the supply chain for drugs, the business was affected in totality. New York Police also clamped down on petty crime, not just big ones, and succeeded in pushing through what came to be known as 'Quality of Life' policing. Many of Giuliani's policies were considered controversial and questions are still raised about how much of the credit for cleaning up New York City should actually be apportioned to him. But I can vouch that during his time and after, I slept soundly at night knowing that my older daughter lived in Harlem and taught in the Bronx, and my younger daughter worked in Manhattan while living in Brooklyn. Giuliani's strategy paid off because he had been able to make the connection between homicide and drugs, guns, broken windows and panhandlers, which may not be apparent but is very real.

When you are out to achieve exceptional success you will have to approach every aspect with a deeper view. The success of a strategy depends on the ability of those who conceive it to see the bigger picture and the interconnected nature of things. Attack a problem with sales by emphasizing on the training and development of the salespeople; fix the attrition issue by improving your badge value; and expand your business not by making your customer list look like Noah's Ark, but by being selective about your customers and knowing which ones, when served preferentially, can deliver the exponential growth you are looking for.

As organizations sprout, some elements of strategic thinking are certainly at play but these are always nested at the top. As the same organizations experience rapid growth, strategic capacity must become fractal; people at all levels must be encouraged to think strategically. Companies do not scale themselves; it is the people who take it to the next step. For a strategy to scale, its implementation needs to enlist people. And people do not necessarily get inspired by strategy that uses impressive analyst reports and histograms and pie charts as crutches. A strategy is most effective when presented as a simple idea that touches a chord and then moves people to action. Paul Polman, presently Chief Executive Officer (CEO) of Unilever, understood this well.

Unilever is regarded as one of the greatest management factories of the world because of the way it grooms its cadre. Yet, when the time came to pick their chief in 2009, Unilever looked to an outsider. Paul Polman had worked practically all his life in Procter & Gamble and had recently moved to Switzerland to work as the Chief Financial Officer (CFO) and Executive Vice President for the Americas at Nestlé. When Polman came on board, Unilever in the West was at best coasting along in markets saturated with soaps, shampoos and ice creams. Paul Polman set a hairy, monstrous goal for the 1,71,000 people working in a slow-growth enterprise. He asked his people to set their eyes on doubling the turnover from 40 billion Euros to 80 billion Euros by 2020. But he also asked for something else. While doubling the revenue, he asked that it be achieved by lowering the carbon footprint to the levels at which they had stood in 2010. When the goal of doubling sales while simultaneously lowering the company's carbon footprint was disseminated among Unilever's employees, suppliers and other stakeholders, it had an electrifying effect. Suddenly, it seemed to be a worthwhile, uplifting goal. But peel the onion and you will see that lowering the carbon footprint means a massive rethink of products, manufacturing systems, supply chain, target markets, the innovative use of information technology and a hundred other things. Suddenly, Unilever was no longer just selling more of the same soaps and shampoos. Unilever employees were no longer a tired lot serving the requirements of a behemoth; they became warriors for the planet. It was Polman's way of waking up Unilever and rallying the troops for unprecedented growth on a markedly different plank.

Polman's thinking exemplifies another, often unseen, characteristic of great strategy: it is not the child of reason; it is an act of emotion.

Emotive thinking, once considered unrelated to business, is actually a very valuable tool and has been the fountainhead of many great ideas that have had generational, irreversible impact. Speaking about emotions, a story about Apple's breakthrough marketing strategy against the century-old IBM that once dominated the computer business is my all-time favourite. IBM was then in its heyday, dominating the personal computer market. The company's tagline at the time was 'Think'. In 1997, Apple was at best a challenger and Steve Jobs decided that apart from other things, Apple's image needed to be strengthened through impactful advertising that encapsulated the core characteristics of the company's products and work ethos. With the help of the American advertising agency TBWA\Chiat\Day, they started a memorable ad campaign with the tagline 'Think Different'. The campaign featured renowned people in history who had changed the course of mankind with their ideas. In television commercials, Apple showed movie clippings from the lives of people like Martin Luther King and Mohandas Karamchand Gandhi, Winston Churchill and Muhammad Ali. The message was clear: 'Think' was no longer good enough. 'Think *Different*' was the new mantra. The campaign worked brilliantly to position Apple as an idea-led, innovative, next-gen company. What I find clever in the Apple commercial is that it used mainly dead people who do not charge modelling fees and do not throw tantrums on production sets. Even today, the campaign remains fresh in people's minds thanks to YouTube. While the ad gets downloaded a million times from YouTube, Apple incurs neither hosting nor broadcast fees.

Strategy is as strategy does, and when it comes to strategy, simple is smart. While great strategy may be created and articulated at higher levels, its execution is successful only when the people executing it connect to it and understand it. When Mahatma Gandhi took on the British empire, all he asked his followers to pursue were two ideas: non-violence and non-cooperation. Non-violence is simple. If you hit me, I will not return the blow. Non-cooperation, in the context of the freedom movement, meant, I will not do what you coerce me to do. These ideas were as naked and simple as the Mahatma himself. That is why, sans embellishment, they were understood and adopted by an entire nation, from the Harrow- and Trinity-educated Jawaharlal Nehru to the illiterate indigo farmers in Champaran, Bihar.

Groups conducting strategy meetings mostly believe that strategy must be sophisticated, complex and beyond average comprehension to look like it's the real stuff. Nothing could be further from the truth, as the Mahatma would tell you and the British would concur.

3

A BAMBOO BRIDGE TO CROSS THE OCEAN

> Successful organizations invariably mimic living beings in designing their infrastructure. The more they incorporate a systemic view, the more evolved and truly scalable they will be.

LIVING BEINGS ARE CHARACTERIZED by the concept of simultaneity. Take an ant, for example. If you observe it move, you will see that it does so with a certain purpose, in a certain direction and at a certain speed. Every little bit of it is coordinated. If you touch the ant, however lightly, its brain registers the event with zero latency at that very instant. Now think of a human being. Like the ant, the human body is simultaneous in all its parts and as a whole. Its various parts perform different functions simultaneously to maintain the balance required for the body to be at peak performance. Information flow in a human being is instantaneous; latency is a sign of paralysis. If

I touch your hand, your brain immediately processes the data and communicates the nature and intensity of the touch to the limb. It also directs your response or reaction. That loop is closed in a matter of milliseconds. It is a highly collaborative system that constantly handles terabytes of 'big data' arriving mostly in unstructured forms. The human system is also designed to deal with redundancy, local healing, isolation in the case of an emergency, and it is capable of learning as it goes along. From another perspective, the human body is governed by perfectly designed infrastructure, one that has evolved with a maximalist view and not a minimalist one.

Successful organizations invariably mimic living beings designing their infrastructure. The more they incorporate a systemic view, the more evolved and truly scalable they will be. While progressive organizations understand the importance of this and build capacity ahead of time, it remains an afterthought to most others during their growth phase. That in itself settles the height of the glass ceiling for the organization. After all, you can cross a bridge only after you have built it.

Organizations that are designed for growth have to think of infrastructure at three distinct but interconnected levels. First, the physical infrastructure. These are your offices, factories, warehouses and retail outlets. Then the intellectual infrastructure. This consists of the enabling systems, processes and methodologies. Above these lies the emotional infrastructure. This involves, among other things, the accessibility of an organization's leaders, how its communities work within the system, its ability to respond to crises, and the propagation of its core vision and values.

If you visualize the three layers, this is what it will look like: the physical at the bottom, the intellectual in the middle, and the emotional on top. Each of these layers must be creative, robust and built ahead of time. They must be seen as critical components of an organization's capacity for the future.

An increasingly important element of infrastructure design, and this is applicable to all three levels, is what we could call the 'digital strategy' of an organization. Early investment in an appropriate information system that mimics a living being's nervous system has boundless advantages. Let us go back to the earlier example of the touch sensation, its reception by the brain and the subsequent completion of the response loop with zero latency, and extend that metaphor to an enterprise you or I may build. For instance, if the supply chain between a factory, or supplier, and retail is not using a zero latency information system, it means higher costs, loss of competitive edge and customer dissatisfaction. In today's world it also has other implications. Many companies depend on the finances they raise from external sources, whether these are a private equity fund, a venture capitalist, a bank, or the public at large. In all such cases, providing accurate, on-demand accounting information is non-negotiable. Imagine an organization that needs to open six offices in six countries. It needs to develop not just the company's ability to produce for and serve global markets, but also a sophisticated information system that must be able to handle complexities like local taxation and currency fluctuation before its books can be closed on demand. Again, in businesses based on retail channels, even in reasonably well-managed ones, pilferage, whether by shoppers or their employees, will easily be 5 to 7 per cent. There may be others that are worse off. If these companies do not have checks in place even in the form of a network of digital cameras that intelligently communicate with a central system, pilferage at any level will eventually bleed them dry.

The intellectual and emotional infrastructure of an organization involves not just its employees and management which an effective intranet can take care of. It is equally about connecting customers with every part of the organization. Ask Marriott International, a leader in the lodging industry. Exploring ways to use technology in order to optimize profit across its properties, increase the efficiency of its selling processes and enable delivery of impeccable service, Marriott 'mapped' the stress levels of the typical traveller. The study revealed that when a guest leaves home, the individual's stress level is high. When he or she reaches airport security, the stress level rises further, and then lowers as the person settles down inside the plane. It goes up again when the plane lands and during the wait at the baggage area, and expands, rises and falls from the time of boarding a taxi to the check-in line at the hotel reception. It reaches the lowest level when the guest finally crashes in the hotel bed. In the case of a person planning a meeting, the stress continues the next day as the person ensures that the meeting room is organized and everything is ready for the attendees to spend a productive day. Then the stress map repeats itself like an electroencephalogram (EEG) graph from check-out to the time when the guest crashes in bed at home.

Accordingly, Marriott focuses on the peak levels in the stress maps and looks for ways to use information technology to reduce the levels at the corresponding points of experience. In the future, Marriott's guests may use an app in a handheld device to check into the hotel before arriving. On arrival they can proceed straight to the room, use their smart phones at the door to enter and, of course, they can order room service before reaching the hotel. People who are planning meetings can use a mobile application to interact with a 'Red Coat', a term used for key support staff, who will respond to their needs and create an elevated meeting experience. The Red Coat can respond to requests for food and beverage, setting up audio-visual systems and even temperature regulation, among other things. The Red Coat is also able to organize the physical infrastructure of the hotel to better the emotional experience of the customer. The unique use of technology has enabled Marriott to deploy a digital strategy that encompasses all three layers of its infrastructure: physical, intellectual and emotional.

For the ultimate visualization of taking a strategic view of infrastructure and proactively investing in creating it, one needs to take a trip to Singapore.

It is common knowledge that in an emergency, the road leading to Singapore's Changi Airport can become a second runway that a 747 jet can land on. All that needs to be done is the rapid removal of flower pots that serve as road dividers. In planning the airport, the administration has taken a long-term view and equipped it for the eventuality of a plane's failure to land because the main runways of Changi Airport have been, for some reason, disabled and the island state has lost its rapid response capability.

The seriousness with which Singapore takes its infrastructure is not limited to an emergency or disaster management. Many people do not know how the sewerage system works in Singapore. Housing in the city predominantly comprises high-rise buildings. Beneath it, is a 48-kilometre tunnel that runs from Kranji in the north of the island country to Changi in the south. There are 60 kilometres of link sewers, a water reclamation plant that can treat 800,000 cubic metres of sewage per day and two pipelines that extend 5 kilometres into the sea to take care of outfall of the excess water. These pipelines rest on the sea bed and are protected from accidental damage by means of anchors. Most importantly, the design is such that the discharge does not get affected even during high tide when the sea actually pushes it back into the pipes. The sewage system is designed to handle capacity and to last against all imaginable threats.

Building capacity for the future prepares an organization for success and equips it with the ability to recover from setbacks. If your vision is to cross an ocean, you won't build a bamboo bridge.

4

THE ELEPHANT CATCHERS

> ‘Unlike an operation to catch rabbits, trapping an elephant calls for expertise over enthusiasm. Those who hunt rabbits are rarely able to rope in elephants.’

MY FATHER USED TO be posted in the mountainous tribal districts of Odisha, and I grew up in places like Koraput, Keonjhar and Ganjam. Many of my schoolmates came from nearby villages and some were from tribal families. In the time I spent with them I learnt a lot about their ways – how they took care of their cows and chickens, how they grew crops, caught fish, and hunted birds and animals. Sometimes, I would go along with them and watch them work, emptying a pond to catch fish trapped in the mud or chasing a full-grown bear to claim its hair, which they believed would cure them of a fever. I heard many stories, too, of other hunts. The ones that fascinated me most were the ones in which big animals were tracked down and brought back alive. From these stories, I learnt quite early on in life that catching small game differs vastly from hunting big animals.

First, a primer on catching small game and the rituals that surround it, the way I remember it from my childhood.

Once or twice a year an electrifying piece of news would make the rounds: that the residents of a particular village were going to go on a hunt the following Sunday. The announcement was an invitation to participate in the excitement of the events to come. Anyone who was male but not an infant could join the expedition. In the approaching days stories of past hunts were retold, with exaggerated claims being made by individuals for themselves or their forefathers. On the appointed Sunday, great excitement would descend on the village as everyone gathered together. When the time was right, the headman, with the blessings of the village priest, led the assembly on their mission. The veterans carried respectable weaponry – a javelin, or a bow and arrows. Others brought whatever they could, from bamboo poles to brooms. These were the hunters. Then there were those with the next level of expertise, the torch-bearers, noise-makers and encirclers. The group proceeded to the forest nearby, then split up to close in from all sides. Led by the noise-makers they began a cacophony that could raise the dead, with drums and cymbals and, for those who did not have these instruments, any household utensils that were at hand. Their task was to create enough disturbance to draw out small animals like rabbits and occasionally a deer that would get frightened and rush about in confusion. All along, the torch-bearers played a multi-utility role: from lighting up the path on the way into the forest to keeping serious danger at bay; sometimes they started a bush fire to drive the animal towards the hunters. At the opportune moment, the hunters would strike and capture the animal. Great joy and much celebration would ensue. At the end of the expedition when the team returned to the village, the meat would be distributed, a local brew consumed, and the episode would become part of folklore, just as others had before it – until the next hunt was announced.

Contrast this with the way wild elephants are caught. It is an expedition of some magnitude and must, therefore, be preceded by intensive planning over a period of time. A pilot party must first track the elephant herd and gather knowledge about its movements. Then another expert group is dispatched to dig an elephantine ditch at a suitable location along the herd's regular route and camouflage it with foliage and undergrowth. When the elephant herd crosses, one of the elephants falls into the ditch. The other members of the herd try to rescue the trapped animal, and after days may leave it to its fate. At this time, a third group of elephant catchers arrives with a couple of specially trained domesticated elephants in tow. The captured elephant is then roped and pulled out with great skill, and coaxed back to the village with the help of the trained elephants. Here, the wild elephant is quarantined, usually in a cage with wooden bars, where the first approaches are made with food and water. Then slowly, over time, it is domesticated and trained by experienced mahouts and the tame elephants. Unlike an operation to catch rabbits, trapping an elephant calls for expertise over enthusiasm.

There is little similarity in purpose and process, from planning to execution, between hunting small game like the rabbit and catching elephants. You catch a rabbit to eat its meat. It has consumptive value but not regenerative value. You don't catch the elephant to eat it; once caught and tamed, it is meant to be an economic resource. While the rewards are great, the risks are very personal, and a failed enterprise can bring grievous injury and may even prove fatal.

Every start-up is somewhat tribal. There is closeness among the initial settlers and everyone participates in everything with great excitement. Yet, before you know it, your business will demand that you move on from catching rabbits to trapping elephants. When you start out, the thought of posting predictable quarter-on-quarter growth figures is quite distant. After all, tribesmen who chase small game do not have to raise funds for the hunt. They do not have to form alliances from across the world, and they do not hire people with the promise of stock options. But as the enterprise grows it is bound to attract external expectations from many quarters. Your customers and clients may begin their relationship with you based on trust and a certain personal connect, but as the initial years go by they begin to build critical dependence on how you manage your internal affairs. They demand process maturity and vertical expertise. They want you to build domain capability and invest in large-deal structuring. They want to know if you will be there five, and even ten, years on and what you are doing to ensure it. You are on the growth trajectory and now you have to think beyond your initial enthusiasm and those first days of heady plans and big ideas.

Such expectations are not strictly external. Sooner or later you have to ask yourself what you are going to do about the future salaries of your present employees. George Zacharias, Chief Strategy and Marketing Officer of Mindtree, one day, showed us a rather poignant slide. It depicted how much money we would need to pay our people as raises over the *next* five years and contrasted it with our income in that time based on the price increase we were managing to get from our existing customers over the *past* five years. It was an ugly picture that told the story eloquently: we would go out of business pretty soon unless we changed the game. In order to simply meet the needs of our own people, who had helped us set up the business and get our initial wins and who would now want to see growth for themselves, we would have to scale. We could no longer be chasing rabbits, that is, the small-change deals, or the five-, ten- or twenty-people projects that would last a year or two. Such deals would not even pay for the average annual salary increase in the company, forget funding capacity-creation essentials like building infrastructure, training and development for our people, and brand-building. We now needed the large deals, the size and predictability of future revenues, and to chase customers who would deliver an annuity-based revenue stream for a long time to come. In short, we needed to capture the elephants. But the problem, as we realized soon enough, starts before the hunt begins: those who hunt rabbits rarely become elephant catchers.

Catching elephants is not just about landing the large deals. It is about all those things that require the ability to handle volume with complexity. Think of the following situations. You want to list overseas, and the current head of finance in your company is unfamiliar with international regulatory issues and at the same time is not good at hiring and managing experts who have the required knowledge. Or, a client asks that you add a boutique capability to your services by buying out their current partner in Prague. This requires re-badging their employees after taking into account legal, human resources (HR) and cultural issues, and the current head of your HR department doesn't know the difference between the French, the Germans and the Czech. Or, consider this: you are used to hiring fresh engineers in hundreds but in the next phase of growth you need to hire a thousand. I could give innumerable examples. All things accounted for, you are looking at a whole new phase in which you absolutely must have experts leading the way. You need the elephant catchers.

Taking such experts on board is fraught with its challenges. Elephant catchers are hard to come by. The best among them almost always work for the king. The renegades and the less efficacious are easy to hire, but they demand fancy money and expensive severance benefits. It takes diligence and huge time commitment to find someone who is good at what he does and is willing to leave the king's service for the challenge of building something from the ground up.

Even if you identify such an individual, it doesn't mean things will automatically fall into place. No one goes to capture a pachyderm on his own, or with just one expert in tow. Usually, elephant catchers work as teams and get hired as such. It may happen that the guy you have hired to pilot the large-deal team brings you a lead, but before anything concrete comes about he wants to hire a domain expert. In addition, he says, he needs to engage an accounting firm and legal counsel because no one in the existing team can make head or tail of the hundred-page Request for Information (RFI) docket. Such a situation can easily get out of hand and add to the woes of the organization instead of leading it forward and upward.

The issue of compensation may also arise. Elephant catchers come at a price that may raise eyebrows and change the status quo in your existing set-up. Then there is the added pressure of adjusting reporting lines. Hiring an elephant catcher and making him report to the 'village chieftain' who has so far only caught rabbits and guineafowl will cause unending pain to the system. The chieftain probably has more stories than scars, more memory than muscles on his aching body, and views the elephant catcher and his team as threats. The elephant catcher looks upon the 'villagers' as amateurs, and they in turn respond with a range of emotions: from sulking to subversive compliance.

Lastly, elephant catchers do not come with a guarantee. In three cases out of four, they may fail. When they do they may try to blame it on the economic slowdown, the inability of the organization to invest in all the paraphernalia they had thought necessary and, of course, the unwillingness of the 'villagers' to change their old ways. And so, before you know it, you have spent lakhs of rupees, perhaps even crores, and have begun to lose faith.

There are great success stories of organizations graduating from small game to large, but they all begin with the fundamental realization that the social contract that brought everyone together in the beginning – with bows and arrows, drums and utensils – no longer works. The social contract that laid the foundation of the village will have to be replaced with one for a city. It is time to step back and rethink the purpose of the organization, and be ready to remodel its structure and functioning. Being able to work future backward by imagining what the customer, supplier and employee of the future, five and even ten years out, will expect from the organization is the perfect starting point.

Every journey comes with its own price. It is better to budget for it than to be taken by surprise. Some of the early settlers, the senior employees, will clearly understand that the company they once started, or joined at its inception, is no longer the same. They will realize that they have to make friends with the elephant catchers and learn some of the skills themselves. These individuals will eventually be able to accelerate their learning process, try new ways of doing things, make a few mistakes and get going. A few will get there after initial protests, and others will get trampled in the ensuing drama. For the first two categories it can be a unique and rewarding experience in personal re-engineering, as well as a great opportunity to renew their social contract with the enterprise as it begins on its next long march. The rest must be left behind to tell stories to their grandchildren.

PART II

SCALING YOUR BUSINESS

5

THE CAT AND DOG DIFFERENTIAL

> ‘The key to winning a customer's business is to be able to connect, and to come across as hungry, willing, genuine, trustworthy and, above all, interesting.’

IT WAS A DREARY, desolate morning late in the winter of 2009. The sky was heavily overcast. It had been raining continuously ever since we had left Cologne in Germany. Mindtree's Europe head, Vishaal Gupta, was driving. I was in the front passenger seat and our co-founder and CEO, Krishnakumar Natarajan (KK), sat at the back. The three of us were going to Amsterdam, Netherlands, across the German border, to call on KPN, a Dutch telecom giant. KPN had recently bought an IT services company named Getronics. Before it was acquired, Getronics had itself bought another IT services company named PinkRoccade. Years ago, Mindtree had done business with PinkRoccade.

That morning, Vishaal was trying to achieve the impossible. He wanted KPN, who did not know us at all, to give us business. Word was they were looking for a partner to provide infrastructure management services. There were three hitches here. First, KPN had not been involved with Mindtree in the past and did not know us except for a cursory name recall based on the PinkRoccade connection. Second, their requirement was in the infrastructure management domain, which Mindtree was just beginning to dabble in. Third, they had issued Request for Proposals (RFP) to Accenture and Infosys. After the RFP submission by the vendors, a team from KPN would visit India for an on-the-ground study of the vendors' capabilities and then take a decision. It was going to be a toss-up between the two companies they had approached; Mindtree was not in the fray at all.

As we crawled forward through the damp grey morning and the inevitable traffic snarl, I was being pesky. I asked Vishaal why on earth Erwin de Bont, the man we were going to see at KPN, should even be meeting us. What could KK and I tell him that would make him sit up and take notice? I was sceptical. Vishaal, as ever, was optimistic, and KK was in between. I needed a real good reason to place before Erwin de Bont that would ensure we got the RFP. Vishaal had no cogent answer, but he was not looking for one. He was simply looking to get the RFP. As is my wont, I wanted to simulate the conversation with Erwin de Bont prior to the meeting to be able to anticipate his state of mind, whatever it may be, and be fully prepared for any eventuality before we met. But, however much I tried, I could not decide on the right approach that would give the man a reason to hear us out. As I thought things over, it occurred to me that internally all of us were feeling let down with what was an unfair situation. We had worked really hard and served PinkRoccade well, yet the business had simply gone away from us.

I thought of the past. When PinkRoccade had wanted an Indian offshore partner, their people had contacted our co-founder and now CFO of Mindtree, Rostow Ravanan. One thing had led to another, a pilot team had arrived, they liked what they saw in us, and work had started. We lacked experience in working with the Dutch but both sides persisted and after some amount of struggle things fell into place. But just as the relationship was about to blossom, PinkRoccade was acquired by Getronics and we had been dumped. We had felt short-changed, but knew well that in the larger scheme of a corporate buy-out, we were collateral damage at best. This morning, however, the unfairness of it all dawned on us again and that is all that mattered. It occured to me that this was the card we would have to play even if it made no difference to Erwin. We had nothing to lose.

'Nothing to lose' is a great concept. It helps the mind to

see possibilities when you are staring at what may look like a full-stop.

When we arrived at the KPN office after what seemed like an unending drive, we were shown into a conference room where Erwin de Bont was waiting. We were aware that he was there out of politeness to listen to our pitch even as his company had made up its mind to choose between the two shortlisted recipients of the RFP. Vishaal had been a pest and Erwin had somehow agreed.

After we shook hands and settled down, I opened the conversation. 'It is the dog that fetched the newspaper for you all these years, but when it is time to feed milk, you are instead choosing the cat,' I told him. Erwin was taken aback with the boldness of the statement and asked me to explain it.

A dog, I told him, is man's ultimate best friend. He is loyal, faithful, obedient, and always happy to please. A cat, on the other hand, is an animal with attitude. It is irreverent to its master and completely useless when compared to a dog. You never expect the cat to fetch you the newspaper or guard the house. In my view, Mindtree was the dog in this situation, and Accenture and Infosys the proverbial cats.

Erwin burst out laughing. He marvelled at the comparison and the audacity with which it had been made. The ice was broken, and at the end of the meeting he agreed to give us the RFP. In the following weeks, Vishaal and our team in India, led by a workhorse named Ram Mohan, worked day and night in preparation for their visit, and when the time came we were ready to put our absolute best foot forward. In the final shortlist, it was Mindtree versus Accenture. Then, Accenture did something utterly strange. They hired an elephant to receive the Getronics team. The group, all Dutch, later told us that they had found it a little over the top.

Both Mindtree and Accenture fought hard on every count. We hard-sold our value proposition: the ease of doing business with us, and our willingness to learn and go the extra mile. In addition, we promised them the three As: Attention, Agility and Access. In the end Getronics seemed to feel more comfortable with the metaphorical dog. They decided to take a chance on us. Within a couple of years they had become Mindtree's No. 1 customer. Since then, every time Erwin and I meet, he makes it a point to remind me of the dog and cat story and we have a hearty laugh. If we had played the card of reason with Erwin that morning in Amsterdam, we probably would have got nowhere. Our competitors for the RFP were 800-pound gorillas in the business. No show of size, domain capability or depth would have cut ice.

Customers do not always give you the first opening and, eventually their business, based entirely on rational thought. An organization that is in its growth phase is usually pitted against much larger entities and needs to think of different, inventive ways to get customers. For such organizations, emotional reasons sometimes work better when knocking on a prospect's door. This is not to underestimate logical reasoning but to underscore the power of emotions. The key to winning the customer's business is to be able to connect, to tunnel a path to their feelings, and to come across as hungry, willing, genuine, trustworthy and, above all, interesting. As a company grows and seeks newer domains, geographies or business models, this adage becomes even more relevant. But for all this to happen, those within the company will first have to get over a mental block.

Imagine that you have been part of the travel industry for a while but now want to add on the financial services vertical to diversify your portfolio. Many people within your company will give you good reasons for such a venture not working out. They may tell you that you have to first invest hugely in building capability in the new vertical before you can get a single meeting with a potential customer, and even then you will probably run the risk of not being 'good enough' to replace existing vendors. They might also tell you that the wisest thing to do is to buy out an existing company in the financial sector to seek domain capability, or that the big buyers have deeply entrenched relationships with your larger competitors and will not be looking for a change. So, why waste time?

In my view, such reasons should not hold you back. The

truth is that while large buyers may be entrenched in long-term contracts, they may still be looking for a change. The reasons can be many. The most common is a change of guard. A new boss may arrive and bring in his own key people. These people may not want to be tied down to existing contracts and will be receptive to new ideas from a fresh quarter. They may be looking at maintaining visible savings as compared to the past and be on the lookout for a quick turnaround of ideas and implementation. Again, due to mandatory audit requirements, large buyers do replace their suppliers periodically but the trick here is to call on them well before the process begins.

This takes me back to something that happened at Mindtree in 2002. By this time we had built up a track record in the manufacturing and travel industries, but we had no idea about financial services and insurance domain. Eager to enter this sector, we called on AIG, an almost hundred-year-old company that today earns more than $64 billion as revenue. When we approached AIG, they were not looking for an IT partner beyond the existing companies they worked with, leave aside the fact that we had no expertise to talk about in the insurance industry. Check with us next year, may be sometime in February, our salesperson was told.

The following year, in February, the salesperson had left Mindtree but she had left behind her sales call reports. The particular sales territory was taken over by a newly recruited business development manager, Ashutosh Shukla. He started by reading up old sales call reports and came across the one citing AIG. Ashutosh picked up the thread from there and called AIG. When his initiative was discussed internally, the first set of discouraging voices spoke up. We don't know insurance and they, AIG, would throw us out even if they granted us a first meeting, he was told. But Ashutosh persisted. He convinced AIG that we deserved to get an RFP. When we did get it, much to our delight, we were told that AIG found our consulting skills and knowledge of e-business impressive. But at the back of our minds, the anxiety about not having insurance domain capability persisted. Interestingly, we found that AIG was not hung up on that. They told us to focus on technology and agreed to bring domain knowledge to the table as long as we were quick to learn. How do you convince someone that you are quick to learn? We showed them our learning processes, we built a prototype course on Insurance 101, we explained to them how we would rope in insurance experts from outside and demonstrated that we knew how to build partnerships with people who knew the domain. Today, AIG remains one of Mindtree's largest customers, thanks to Ashutosh Shukla, who opened the door.

While we won over AIG through persistence, a completely different approach worked for us when we decided to try our luck in the banking sector. Banking is a super-specialized area and it wasn't easy for us to get an opening until I met Ken Wilcox, at the time CEO of Silicon Valley Bank, quite by chance. Ken was in India, getting a feel of the start-up scene because Silicon Valley Bank works mostly with start-ups and entrepreneurial companies. After the meeting, Ken suggested I meet his CIO, Dave Webb. During the subsequent meeting with Dave, I told him that we wanted to do business with banks and no one would open the door for us. Would Silicon Valley Bank be our 'angel customer'? I told him that we were looking at listing the company soon and having Silicon Valley Bank as a marquee name on our list of customers would be an additional favour. This time it was about appealing to the altruistic side of the customer and being open and honest about being the underdog. Dave Webb agreed to take us in. Mindtree's relationship with the bank has been great over all these years, and even as Ken and Dave have moved on, in our minds they remain angels.

So each time someone tells you there is no real reason for you to be invited to the party, remember my story about the cat and the dog, and remember that there are people like Erwin de Bont and Dave Webb who like to do business with the new kid on the block. Every time someone says you have no domain knowledge and track record, remember what happened to us with AIG. And, finally, look for what you may have in common with the customer beyond your expected capabilities and use it to create the connect, as we did with Silicon Valley Bank.

Silicon Valley Bank is not just a bank. It is a bank for start-ups and entrepreneurs, and they liked us as a start-up story even before they liked us as a software services partner.

6

OF HUNTERS, FARMERS, GRIZZLIES AND SKUNKS

> "Sales is not witchcraft. It is a science as much as it is an art, and must be managed with the same discipline as product development, manufacturing and servicing."

PETER D'SOUZA WAS VERY pleased with his initial success. The first big customer came his way thanks to a reference from an existing customer. Peter, a technical person with some background in sales support, got an RFP. He dazzled the evaluation committee in comparison to the competition, who had fielded salespeople who lacked depth of knowledge. Business came in easily enough but executing it took all of Peter's time, leaving him with no resources to find and capture the next big customer.

Peter's company needed to win more and to win in new markets. The venture capitalist who had funded him was clear

– Peter must go all out to get in more marquee names and new logo wins so that the company could avoid overdependence on a slew of small customers and just one big account. That was the only way for a start-up like Peter's to get second-round investors interested. It was time for Peter to expand the sales force and get in the rainmakers. Peter asked a headhunter to scout for candidates and was pleasantly surprised with the profusion of applications that flew in. One looked better than the other. After all, who can spice up résumés better than salespeople? Peter finally hired a high-profile sales guy and the man suggested that New York City would be a good base as the company had no existing business there. As time went by, Peter realized much to his horror that the sales guy was really a grizzly.

If you have ever watched a National Geographic episode on the life of the grizzly bear or of migrating salmons, you will immediately know what I am talking about. The grizzly is an impressive, immensely powerful animal, but a lazy hunter. One of the grizzly's favourite foods is salmon. By one of nature's innumerable miracles, grizzly bears know instinctively the spawning season of migrating salmons, during which the fish, in large and sumptuous schools (and by yet another of nature's marvels) arduously travel upstream to the very same point where they were once spawned. Along the way come shallow waterfalls and rapids, and the fish must jump out of the water and literally scale rocks to resume their onward journey. The grizzly, hungry after months of hibernation, simply positions itself along the river at a vantage point and waits for the fish to appear in mid-air on their 'climb'. It makes absolutely no effort to go after the hurtling fish; the fish simply land in the bear's jaws. At the appropriate moment, all the grizzly needs to do is to open its mouth.

Peter's New York sales guy sat in the office, checking his inbox all day and, in between coffee breaks, cracked popular jokes and complained about the salmons not showing up. Six months passed in the blink of an eye. The man hadn't produced anything. By then, Peter's company was down by $500,000, which included, apart from the man's fixed salary, the joining bonus given to him on day one, the compensation amount for the commission he had forgone in the previous company when he joined Peter, a guaranteed component of the (unearned) sales commission for the first year, and sundry expenses that he had incurred. Peter was at his wit's end. He had never handled a grizzly before. Not knowing where to turn for advice, he spoke to the headhunter again. She explained that the problem with companies like Peter's was that they expected results all too quickly. 'Heavy hitters' must be given time, she said. The grizzly was a big-deal guy. He needed to have the supporting lead-generation machinery, he needed trade-show participation and footfalls before the big ones would land. Have patience, Peter was told. Six more months, and the bear was still on the rocks. The salmon never came.

This time Peter did not sit still. Determined to enlarge his sales force, he hired two much younger, more affordable people and posted them in another city where he had at least a couple of referenceable customers. These two did a better job than he had expected of opening new accounts, but one of the two turned out to be an over-enthusiastic small-deal getter. Each time he brought in a $50,000 deal, he made a show of it. He claimed that the account was very strategic, that this one order was just the beginning, and so on and so forth. Sometimes he also picked up customers who were not right for the company, irrespective of the size of the deal. This salesperson was hell-bent on getting his commission and in the process he brought in skunks. In the absence of an account qualification process, by the time the system realized it, the skunk had already been brought in. He hoped, perhaps, that when ingested the skunk would, by some miracle, taste like free-ranging chicken, or by that time he would probably have switched jobs.

Peter was at his wits' end, unable to fathom where he was going wrong every time. What was the trick he was missing?

He had a heart-to-heart chat with his very supportive venture capitalist, who told him that the problem was that Peter was not a sales manager. The need of the hour was a senior person who could put in place a sales strategy from which the sales plan and then a sales organization would emerge. That, in turn, would determine the kind of salespeople Peter's company should hire. However talented a team of salespeople might be in the art of hooking a customer, selling and sales management are very nuanced and, in their own way, very evolved. An organization that wants to scale its operations, and get in the big business that is essential for sustained growth, must start by professionalizing its sales engine.

In the following weeks, word went out among the investor community. Leads came through, one reference led to another, and that is how Peter got introduced to Joelle Smith and hired her. Over the next six months, Joelle systematically turned the situation around and helped the enterprise's growth trajectory move sharply north. Along the way, she taught Peter a few principles about the sales function that organizations looking to break through the clouds would find immensely valuable.

When you look at the world today, Philip Kotler's 4Ps (Product, Price, Place and Promotion) look very basic. The way verticals have emerged, and within them sub-verticals, has brought about a transformation in traditional ideas of customer segmentation. The creation of sophisticated sales management tools, such as salesforce.com, and the use of analytics to discover the real customer for a product and identify unmet needs, have come to mean that creating an effective sales organization is no longer about entrepreneurial common sense. All successful entrepreneurs are, at some level, salesmen. In the beginning they must sell like hell, but building on and sustaining that initial sales thrust and creating a heaven requires an expert. What Joelle brought to the organization was not old-world persistence, charm and hustle; it was expertise.

Watching the way she operated, Peter learnt that the foremost thing to remember in the creation of a sales force of worth is that all salespeople are not the same. Just as there are the ones to be wary of, like the grizzlies and those who end up inviting in skunks, there are also those who will add great value to the enterprise when employed intelligently.

There are those who are extremely good at finding new opportunities. They can strike up an engaging conversation with a stranger on board a bumpy flight, exchange business cards and close deals in two meetings. Throw them in an alien territory and they will quickly map the place, figure out where the prospects are and plan their moves accordingly. Show them the competition and they will go all out to fight until the end. They enjoy obstacles and thrive on overcoming challenges. With their skills they can literally take the meat out of the lion's mouth. But once they convert a prospect into a customer, these people gradually lose interest. They are good at opening doors but not at slowly, steadily building a relationship. They are intelligent, intuitive and hardworking, but they are not necessarily problem-solvers. They get bored easily and seek variety. These people can be called the hunters.

Then there are those who are not good at opening new accounts, do not like cold-calling and prospecting, and are out of their depth in fiercely competitive situations. But once you land them in an existing customer account they effortlessly create long-term relationships. They easily take on the role of a trusted advisor to the client and can get the company into the consideration set well before the formal contracting process begins. These are the farmers.

A growing organization needs both the hunter and the farmer, and the first task of the organization's leaders is to place the right people in the right positions. Prospecting, qualifying, selling and closing a deal are exhilarating experiences. It is amazing how an entire organization gets galvanized when it is make-or-break time and the prospective customer has whittled down the longlist to just you and your opponent. Everyone pitches in and then, as the hard work pays off, you land the deal and get the customer. Then months go by, and sometimes years, and you realize that while you have the customer's logo on your corporate presentation and some business continues to come in from them, the lion's share of their business is going to your competition, who is making deeper inroads by the day. Your people are doing the niche and sometimes more difficult work, while the competition is better spread out where the volume of the business is larger, and their margins at an account level are better than yours. This is a classic case of the inability to mine the account after initial success. Just as you need the first-rate, hungry, lean, combative hunters to win new logos, you also need the steady farmers who will cross-sell other products and services, seek adjacency while exploring customer needs and make the relationship stick.

Every enterprise that meets with sales success in the initial years faces a peculiar problem as it gets to the next level. The best salesmen, the star performers who opened the doors and brought in the deals, don't want to sell anymore. They want to be managers. They think the key to their professional growth is supervising other salespeople. This is a slippery idea. Most successful salespeople are individual professional contributors and underestimate the complexity of sales management that involves strategic thinking and people-management skills. When they become sales managers, they begin to find cold-calling, the pivot of the sales juggernaut, below their dignity. Now you have a strange situation. There are two individuals doing the job that one used to do before, with one simply sitting on the other's head. This is a more marked problem among Indians who, for cultural reasons, find comfort in status and hierarchy. Personal selling capability is a great skill. When you have reached the stage at which your enterprise is ready to break out, it will be important to remember this and remind your key salespeople of their core skill and its worth.

Just as you need to encourage good salespeople to continue to sell rather than become supervisors, you also need to watch out against creating accidental 'account managers'. This happens when, for instance, a successful delivery guy in a software company, or a creative person in an ad agency, is put in charge of a particular account because he delivers well and has developed a relationship of trust with a client. Propping up a likeable guy in a customer account to manage it may see incremental success but is unlikely to create breakthroughs. Such people are seldom equipped to strategize about account mining, building and following through on an account plan, creating account-specific marketing plans, or pushing back clients and questioning their demands (good guys don't do that, right?). Even though it does not seem apparent, you may end up wasting a good professional by giving him a responsibility he is not inherently suited for.

Whatever the composition of your sales force, to get it to perform to its maximum potential, it is necessary to ask every salesperson for his sales vision for the territory or account in question and then go about seeking wins. The sales vision must go beyond hunting for opportunities in pure monetary terms. It is important for every individual on the force to outline qualitative strategies: What is the overall competitive objective? What will I sell, to whom and why? Who will I not sell to and what will I not sell? What about market share and establishing referenceability? What about the profitability of the sale? How will I imprint my company's reputation beyond winning this one deal?

Flowing from the cumulative sales vision at the company level comes the need to establish a formal sales training programme and, over time, as the enterprise scales, a centralized task force that keeps salespeople well-trained at all times. It is extremely important to have a well-informed sales force that understands the company and its products and services, and does not make unfounded claims. The more your sales force expands, the more the need to keep all levels of the team trained and informed. Conversely, it is crucial to invest in a good information system that scientifically analyses sales data so that at no point do the management and personnel lose sight of the central sales vision. The key questions to ask here are: Where are we winning and where are we losing? What is the deal flow? How do we build predictability of the sales process?

In the end, Peter D'Souza understood well that sales is not witchcraft; it is a science just as much as it is an art. It must be managed with the same discipline as product development, manufacturing and servicing. A sales organization that is built right can alone scale contribute to the success of the organization.

7

MARRIAGES OF CONVENIENCE

> 'As in all walks of life, in business, too, relationship choices have consequences. If you seek a marriage of convenience, do so with your eyes open and always be aware that it just might become an unholy alliance.'

A GROUP OF THREE friends I knew had set up their own IT services business around the same time that we started Mindtree. All three had a predominantly technical background. One of them lived in the US and owned a company there, for which he sourced business from a customer he knew well from past association. The work was then sub-contracted to his two friends in India. These two friends set up the Indian entity largely with their own resources, built all the infrastructure, hired the employees, set up the processes and executed the work.

When I visited them and saw their operation, I noticed two things. One, the Indian company was overly dependent on the US outfit, which in turn was reliant on a single customer. Two, the Indian company was not building any sales capability to acquire new customers. The two friends in India saw no urgency in doing this. They also felt that an effort to build a sales force and scout for new business would seem like an act of disloyalty to the third partner. For now, business was coming in. Why rock the boat, they reasoned.

Unfortunately, within the next couple of years, the single large customer of their counterpart in the US went belly-up, causing the Indian operations to dwindle and, finally, to be sold off.

As companies enter their growth phase, they inevitably need a few strategic relationships that work like a booster rocket. But the choices they make in the process have consequences. At Mindtree, we were able to escape the situation our friends suffered because we have always been wary of over-dependence on one or two customers. In every quarter, since our inception, we tracked the percentage of business we got from our ten leading customers. It helps us to see early signals of how our business may be impacted. It also forces upon us the discipline of getting out there to find new customers so that if something happens to one large customer we always have room to recover. In the same way that we track this metric, I often find large customers wanting to know what percentage of our business depends on them. They do not like that number to exceed a certain threshold because it involves a reverse risk.

Yet, while we at Mindtree have done a good job of de-risking our over-dependence on a small set of customers, we have made the mistake of carrying many small customers into the second phase of our growth in the post-IPO period. In retrospect, we should have been more selective. There are dangers of prolonging relationships with small customers beyond a point. An account-wise analysis we had once conducted of customer satisfaction, and parallely of employee satisfaction among our people working on these accounts in the same period of time, brought out an interesting aspect. The satisfaction level of a customer was inversely related to the size of their project with us. At the same time, projects that remained small over the years showed relatively lower employee satisfaction because people working on them felt stagnated.

While every customer is important to a company, a growing organization must determine a set of parameters to ascertain 'mutual fit'. It is important for growing companies to ask themselves critical questions at regular intervals: How many of our customers think that the alliance has been a positive strategic move on their part? What special things are we doing for those who think this way about us? What are the customers doing to ensure they keep working with us? If the answers are not forthcoming, it is necessary to have an open conversation both internally and with the customer. Just as over-dependence on a customer is not desirable, sub-optimal relationships are not good either.

For a company wanting to scale, the quest for volume business sometimes comes at the cost of diluting the core purpose for which it was built. Take the example of Mindtree's efforts to become a GE Global Development Centre. There was a time when GE was sourcing half a billion dollars of software services from top Indian IT companies. Quite understandably, for an upcoming company like us, becoming a 'GE partner' was a dream. Doing business with GE was a huge learning opportunity. After all, GE had pioneered outsourcing to India way back in the early 90s and, as a result, they had great process maturity. Working with GE could bring about rapid growth for a company like Mindtree. Scalability was important to GE as well. A small operation with an Indian partner would not attract the attention of GE's own customers, or be worth top management reviews or a visit by a GE executive. To be selected as a GE partner preceded a long and tough qualification process. We went through it successfully and when we finally made the cut there was obviously much to rejoice about. Except, in the meantime, GE had changed its business model. It no longer required its new partners to own the work to be executed by them; it simply required them to own the infrastructure and provide the 'resources', that is, the people, to get the job done. GE would then co-locate their employees who would manage the centre.

Accordingly, once Mindtree set up the place and provided the workforce, GE managers moved in. They became the interface with GE customers, they allocated the work, did the project reviews and, in reality, managed Mindtree's workforce. It was not that GE did not tell us all this in the beginning. Rather, it was we who had hoped that the arrangement would be a foot in the door for us. We had been sure that, very soon, they would find us mature and capable enough to manage the day-to-day operations on our own, as they had done with their older partners in India. It took us some time to understand that it was no longer going to be the case.

The GE deal happened just before our IPO. At the time we were a $100 million company. To prospective investors GE was a marquee account and would ensure new business and steady revenue streams for us. But we took a long, deep breath and asked ourselves a few hard questions. Primary among these was: Did we want to be just a resource provider? There is nothing wrong with being one, but that wasn't what we had set out to do. Also, for a software services company, employees are everything. If the customer directly engages with our people, while we as a company remain pure intermediaries, how would we build employee loyalty to Mindtree?

Sometimes, when you look at opportunities to grow your organization's business, volume is not the issue; it is the business model that is. As in all walks of life, in business, too, relationship choices have consequences. Confronted with an unhappy situation, many companies find it difficult to end the association. It is important to remember that a clean divorce is better than an incompatible, and eventually messy, marriage. In life and in business, being strategic sometimes means having the ability to let go.

In this case, after considerable thought, we decided to disengage. Fortunately, the process of ramping down was done amicably. GE understood that our paths were divergent and hence the best thing to do was to part ways.

■

Sometimes large potential customers feel that a relationship will be more secure, and hence 'strategic', if the partner is open to structuring a joint venture (JV) company which then gets the business. At the time of negotiations, enough and more justifications are offered as to why a JV is the way to go. The most common argument is that the customer has valuable intellectual property and a JV will give more scope to both sides to use this well. What most people do not realize is that a JV is a legal nightmare. It imposes a whole set of legal and regulatory obligations as well as a complex taxation framework that either side may not know about. It is a mistaken notion that, by itself, the formation of a joint venture makes business relations strategic and secure. Managing a JV is fulltime work and often results in overshadowing the real purpose for which it was created.

Sometimes, a JV becomes the preferred route, the convenient arrangement, for a different reason. In India, even after the laws relating to Foreign Direct Investment (FDI) have been altered, restrictions remain in certain sectors of our economy. Indian companies agree to a JV knowing that it may offer no significant value but in the hope that in due time, when the laws change, the foreign entity will hand over the reins to the Indian partner at a premium. Wipro Chairman Azim Premji has a pet phrase for this. He calls it, 'Escort services.' Before risking their future with something like this, companies must keep in mind that this kind of alliance is for the big boys and not for small or mid-size companies.

When a company in the pre-IPO stage is scouting for business, a prospective buyer often asks for a share of the equity in exchange for business. It is rationalized as the cost of sourcing and justified as the value of the logo and the promise of getting future business, since all these improve the valuation of the company in the stock market. In the event that the company's stock does well after the IPO, the customer can make a killing. At Mindtree, we made two such deals. They did give us a certain fillip but, in hindsight, I don't think we would want to get into similar deals again. The reason for exercising caution is that when the buyer is a large entity, the part of the organization that gives business and the part that executes the equity deal are usually separate and have different yardsticks of measure. After the deal is struck, they will go their own ways, and the acquired company will be left to struggle with the fact that it is considered just another vendor in search of business and must come to every subsequent RFP to compete on merits. There is no chance of receiving preferential treatment even though it has given away its equity. Worse, thanks to the frequent reorganizations that large companies go through, the people who were conducting the business may soon be replaced by new recruits. Now the equity that was sold off has no relevance at all; no one will remember the gain they might have made from acquiring it.

If giving away equity in exchange for business is unavoidable, it must be done after great thought and consideration. There are a few things to keep in mind in such situations. When you structure the equity for a business deal you need to defend the need for fair value and never discount your share price. Negotiate such that the shares accrue only when a certain volume of business has happened. In other words, ensure that it is revenue-linked. Take expert help and do not be shy to get a lawyer on your side.

In saying this, I am not writing off JVs altogether. If it makes good business sense, parting with equity is not always a bad idea. All I am saying is ensure there is a good reason to take this step, seek expert help in structuring the deal, hold aloft examples of failed arrangements elsewhere and, finally, do what you wish to do with your eyes open. In choosing a relationship, if the promise of the future comes with a price tag, the company must look at the cost of ownership in its entirety and not sacrifice its future for the sake of the present. If you seek a marriage of convenience, always be aware that it just might become an unholy alliance.

8

THE M&A MYTHS

> 'When managers propose mergers and acquisitions, the important thing is to ensure that they are doing it for the right reasons, and not because they have run out of ideas on how to grow their business organically, or are fatigued and now see a merger or an acquisition as an easy way out.'

OVER THE YEARS AT Mindtree, the board understood that I had a hawkish position on the issue of mergers and acquisitions (M&As). A co-founder, Scott Staples, summed up my attitude well: 'Subroto does not like the idea of someone peeing in his pool.'

Yes, I do believe most mergers and acquisitions are ultimately about allowing other people to pee in your pool. But despite my negative feelings towards the idea, at Mindtree we made at least one significant acquisition that worked out well for us. There was also one, however, that was like a near-death experience and could have completely destroyed the organization we had built with the sweat of our brows.

The first time we acquired a company was when we were struggling to build a SAP practice for ourselves because our most significant customer at the time wanted us to have SAP capability. Building SAP capability is not easy. SAP-proficient people don't join you unless you have a customer-funded project and customers don't give you work unless you have these people on board. Faced with a catch-22 situation, we looked around and acquired a small SAP outfit in Delhi. It had four young co-founders. The main entrepreneur was stationed in Delhi and the other three did business in the US. None of the people we took on when we acquired the outfit are with Mindtree today, except the front office receptionist. The founders went their ways in quick succession after cashing in. Most of the customer engagements the company had were at the tactical level even though their customers were large, but the acquired entity was so marginal in the customers' overall business that we didn't really benefit. The company had some intellectual property, which we overvalued; today no one knows where that code is lying in Mindtree. Initially, we spent enormous amounts of energy trying to retain the original founders, assuring them that they could build the business without fetters, that they could be a start-up within a start-up. It did not work.

We learned two valuable lessons from this acquisition.

First, the founders never stay, do whatever you may. Paying money as a retention bonus is a throwaway. It gives you false assurance that key people may stay to create new synergies and help in the process of integration. The sad thing about M&As is that the so-called key people get large payouts that very often make them lazy and they lose interest in working with the same level of commitment as before.

Second, if the founders of the acquired unit hit a glass ceiling and could not grow their company beyond their current situation, it is unlikely they would do any better in the changed scenario. Smaller companies often cite resource constraints as the roadblocks they couldn't get past and argue that they will be successful once acquired by a larger entity but more often than not this does not happen.

At Mindtree, we had two businesses in the beginning: IT services, which focused on building enterprise applications, and R&D services, which worked with product companies. The SAP acquisition had been for the former. After this, in every strategy conversation, the R&D folks proposed the acquisition of a new company in their area. It seemed to be seen as the panacea for all ills, from falling revenues to loss of orders. Finally, we made another insignificant acquisition. This was an R&D outfit started by a bunch of techies who had built a small product of sorts; they were geeks and they were happy to be taken over. They came cheap, and at our end most people believed that the acquisition would significantly stretch our capacity to deliver more complete solutions. It was a low-cost, low-risk acquisition. What could go wrong? But small and cheap acquisitions lack critical mass, and because of their size the leadership of the acquiring company loses interest in them after taking over. After the initial hoopla the acquired company is left to its own devices or ignored, in the process exacerbating the alienation of people who come in.

Why do managers ask for M&As? Quite often they convince themselves and others about the 'strategic nature' of a deal, the creation of great new synergies, of costs evening out as the benefits of scale kick in, and other such stuff. This is mostly smoke. The important thing is to ensure that these managers have not run out of ideas on how to grow their business organically, or are fatigued and now see a merger or an acquisition as an easy way out.

Even when small and inexpensive deals are proposed, it is important to keep in mind that making things work in an acquisitions deal, whether big or small, consumes the same amount of energy.

Then there is the issue of managing 'key employee' expectations. Each time you acquire an entity, there will inevitably be a set of employees who come in with fancy salaries and flaunt big designations (which is how they drove things to the ground before you bought them out). They now want a giant raise and many new benefits as a result of the merger. They negotiate well for themselves but don't necessarily do so for the larger base of their employees. The latter come in as children who now have a wealthier uncle and aunt adopting them. The only thing that may excite them about the merger is the prospect of a salary hike. If you offer a salary hike to all the employees, the cost-benefit equation of the M&A deal will fly out of the window. If you are unable to fit the acquired employees into your compensation-and-benefit structure, they will feel left in the lurch and the process of integration will suffer. If you retain their privileges, you will hurt your own people. Either way, you get grumpy kids!

Every M&A is meant to go through some level of 'due diligence' to uncover tell-tale signs against proceeding with the deal. If the acquisition is of a private company, the due diligence process is similar to the preparatory stages of an arranged marriage. You can ask informal, probing questions to related businesses or people. However, if it is a listed company, the law prevents you from digging beyond the information that is publicly available. The truth is that very few managers have the intuitive capability, the nose, as it were, to smell things out. Sometimes, people who do the due diligence start with the mindset that the deal is final and unstoppable and wish that nothing awkward surfaces, to the extent that if something is amiss they might not even spot it. And sometimes even if there is something fishy, the information can be so abstract that most managers would have a hard time citing it as a reason for calling off a deal.

During the days when we were looking for a SAP 'shop', a rival of ours was in the process of selling their SAP company. Naturally, it came up for our consideration. Some doubts arose. The rival had acquired the company just a couple of years back, terming it a 'boutique' acquisition. Why then were they selling it so soon? Our people justified this by saying that equations between two companies could always change, that we should not get so nitpicky, and so forth. As the time came for the final call to be made, I went to Los Angeles to meet the top management of the company on offer. After an elaborate conversation, I had just one question left to ask: Was anyone in the top management of the organization related to anyone within it? There was a moment of uncomfortable silence. Then the CEO clarified that his wife was the head of their HR department. I flinched. Now, you can argue that there is absolutely nothing wrong with this and that one should not be judgemental. But an M&A is a game of judgement. You should prefer to err on the side of caution if you do not want to waste your money. If the CEO's wife is the HR head, which employee in his right senses would ever raise an uncomfortable issue of any kind? That apart, there are two functions in any progressive company that must play the role of corporate guardian, particularly when it comes to saving a company from an errant CEO. These two functions are finance and HR. If a CEO crosses the line, it is the responsibility of the heads of finance and HR to exercise the responsibility of dissent and, if that fails, to take up the matter with the board. This is least likely to happen if the CEO and the head of HR are related to each other. Taking all things into consideration, we walked out of the deal.

It wasn't much later that we walked into another deal and, this time, the due diligence business did not quite work. We bought over the Indian R&D arm of a leading Japanese company with the idea of rolling out a smartphone that was played up as a game changer. We were very happy with the deal. We had paid just $5 million with an on-going revenue stream from the seller that would make the deal pay for itself within the first year. Our own R&D department had all the design experience except that one last bit that the acquired entity had always done for the parent unit in Japan. The perceived synergy was mind-blowing.

While the deal went through, a series of uncomfortable issues started surfacing soon after the acquisition. These invariably pointed to the top. The only person who had full knowledge of any matter in the acquired entity was the head of the R&D unit and we were fully aware of the excessive dependence on that one man. We explained it by saying that, after all, it was the critical R&D arm of a Japanese company and confidentiality was paramount. This was a company with a different culture from ours, we reasoned, so let's not look for skeletons where none may exist. But that one waiver led us into deeper, murkier waters. Issues of personal integrity and evidence of laxity in governance issues inevitably led to the contamination of the planning process, procurement decisions, the performance appraisal mechanism and every other area of work.

Initially we thought that needling the top man whenever prickly issues came to the surface could jeopardize the bet-all product rollout that was due in a few months. When we found the unit indulging in practices that differed from Mindtree's established processes, our people felt uncomfortable about taking it up with the head of the acquired unit. The pressure to make the deal work was coupled with the hope that we would straighten things out once the product rolled out. But that never happened. The product was a dud.

Meanwhile, every few days a new issue surfaced. The head of the unit we had acquired and his deputy were childhood friends and the two had worked together for many years. This was common knowledge. What we didn't know was that the outfit used to hire employees from a placement company run by the deputy. Often, prospective employees were asked to come in as contractors on the payroll of the placement company for a few months before being hired. When we enquired, the head of the unit denied any knowledge of the third party transaction by his deputy who, in the meantime, had quit.

Finally, matters got worse as some revelations concerned the head himself. The contract we had signed for the buy-out required us to honour the existing employment conditions of senior employees of the Japanese company. We said, yes, of course. Soon after the takeover, someone from our HR unearthed an earlier arrangement that allowed the head of the unit to lease a car from his own driver and, that too, at three times the market price! Technically it could be explained away, but morally it was stinking fish. The lesson from this was huge. It does not take technology to create great things, it takes people, and the people we had brought in had a completely different way of looking at governance.

Every time these issues surfaced, there was excitement among our people. They were like schoolchildren who were continuously finding worms in their newfound cousin's drawers and, more than anything else, wanted to see how we, the parents, would react. Finally, one day, we had to bite the bullet and close the outfit but the damage caused was massive. Mindtree had to write off millions of dollars, hundreds of people were asked to leave, including the head of the acquired unit, and a series of convulsions gripped Mindtree's board along with a large management shakeout to boot. Our stock plummeted to one-third its price and the *Economic Times* ran a front-page story with the caption: 'Mindtree Faces Uncertain Future'.

Most management literature will tell you that 90 per cent of M&As do not work. They are value-destructive, and in most cases culture-dilutive. Yet, when entered into conservatively, with good reason and extensive involvement of the top management after the merger, M&As can be successful. They can unlock hidden cost-benefits by expanding operations, allow companies to take newer offerings to existing customers, or add a new domain or geography to its business. The tragedy is that in a majority of M&A proposals, the people driving the deal argue that there is greater than 70 per cent chance of it succeeding. An effort to inform them about the reality, and save the organization a lot of hassle in the process, is like preaching celibacy to a teenager.

9

VALUE, VALUATION & THE ROLL UP KIDS

> 'If anyone tries to show you a path to double or treble your company's valuation overnight, don't get taken in. Life is about constant growth, but any unnatural growth is inherently destructive.'

IN 2005, A COUPLE of years ahead of Mindtree's public issue, a gentleman from a leading newspaper came to see me. He wasn't a journalist, nor was he from the advertisements division of the publication. He was, he said, from a specially formed group within the newspaper that carved out deals for small and medium companies in exchange for equity.

I was intrigued.

He explained that since organizations in their initial stages can't afford to buy advertisement space in a national newspaper such as the one he represented, his paper was providing advertising space at a concessional tariff for such companies in exchange for equity.

But we do not advertise, I said. Why would a software services business, focused almost entirely on the Western market, advertise in a national daily? In any case, new customers did not come to us through advertising.

At the time of the meeting, Mindtree was at a stage when business came to us primarily by word of mouth. One happy customer took us to another. We were too small to participate in industry events and trade shows, or to attract the attention of analysts and large-deal advisors. And here was a man telling me to buy advertising space at a so-called discount, and in exchange he was asking me to give him a portion of our equity. I offered him a cup of tea and explained to him that we would never give away equity for a discount in exchange of goods and services because it was, simply, unwise.

Why do we invest our hard-earned money and build businesses? We do so because we think that the value of the money invested in the business will appreciate manifold and certainly provide a much higher rate of return than if it were sitting in a bank. That being the case, if my business genuinely needed advertising, would it not be cheaper to borrow the money from a bank to buy that advertising space, discount or no discount, than to give away equity for it? It made no sense to me, I told him.

In reply, he told me something that really took me by surprise. He said companies that agreed to be part of the programme would be given more editorial coverage and in the event of any negative news involving the company the news desk could be asked to go easy on the organization, though this could not always be guaranteed. Even as the proposition raised questions in my mind on ethical grounds, it wasn't for me to sit in judgement. I had my own business to mind. No, thank you, I told him.

Years later, I am thankful that I knew how to treat my equity with respect. Many entrepreneurs do not, and they fritter it away because they think the idea of interest-free cash is more valuable than equity. If you build a company of some consequence your equity is, in reality, significantly more valuable than cash.

At one time, in Silicon Valley, it was quite commonplace for real-estate owners and other service providers to offer space in exchange for a company's equity. Sometimes customers demanded a portion of the equity while committing to provide volume business. The joke in Silicon Valley was that even your barber asked to be paid, at least in part, with a portion of your equity. This was so because many first-time entrepreneurs raised money from venture capitalists. Think of this situation: I am the venture capitalist. I give you ₹100 for a 25 per cent stake in your organization. Now the balance 75 per cent is automatically valued at ₹300. It is you who has the idea behind the company and the ability to execute the idea, not me, the venture capitalist – but you do not have ₹300 to invest in your 75 per cent of the ownership. So I tell you that you pay for it with your sweat and it will accrue to you in five annual installments. In the process, I make sure that you will be around for five years and have skin in the game.

The really interesting part begins now. Over the next five years, as you execute your idea and paying customers come in, the business grows. Other investors take notice of it and one comes along with a proposal: for a 10 per cent stake in the company, he will now pay ₹1000! This basically means that your valuation has increased two and a half times the original ₹400 and the new investor is asking the current owners – your original venture capitalist and you – to 'dilute' your ownership by 10 per cent each and make way for him. So there are three owners now – one who owns 22.5 per cent of the equity, one 67.5 per cent, and a new one who owns 10 per cent. The latest valuation of your business is now the baseline for the next set of investors who may come during the initial public offering. In this process of progressive increase in valuation – assuming, of course, that the company is doing well and there is investor interest – a piece of the pie becomes very attractive.

Consider what happened at Mindtree. Ten founders started the company in 1999. We pooled in our personal savings and issued out shares to ourselves at a face value of ₹2 per share. Then came two initial venture capitalists, Walden International from the US and Global Technology Ventures from India. We issued 45 per cent of the total equity of the company to them. They paid us ₹41 per share, a premium of ₹39 over the original ₹2. In the bargain, we raised $9.5 million. In 2001, we went in for a second round of funding. This time, Capital International, the new investor, was issued stock at ₹100 per equity share. Finally, in 2007, Mindtree was listed in the stock market at a price of ₹425 per share. So, assuming a company is managed well and the overall market sentiment is good, the price of shares will always appreciate. In 2012, Walden, our original venture capitalist sold their ownership at ₹610 a share. Now you can see how the value of the equity changed from ₹2 to ₹610 in a matter of thirteen years!

It is true that the value of a company's shares depends on a variety of things and what happened with Mindtree might not happen with another company. But the overall principle remains the same. Even if the eventual valuation of a company's equity is half, or a quarter, of that of Mindtree, frittering it away to secure cheaper office space or to buy advertising in a newspaper is an unwise thing to do. It is a terribly expensive way of doing business. You can borrow money to pay for something your business really needs and repay it with interest. That will be far cheaper than giving away equity.

The sustainable valuation of an enterprise is a function of many things. Chief among them are the quality of the management team, the customer base, the predictability of the revenue stream and, of course, corporate governance. The stock market keeps fluctuating, but if the leaders in the organization are focused on building value, enhanced valuation always follows. Sometimes people mistakenly believe in artificial ways of raising the value of an enterprise or using quick-fix financial engineering, but the investor world is sophisticated enough to be able to separate the grain from the chaff.

■

It was 1999, the heady times of the dot-com bubble, when financial engineering overwhelmed hard work. Quite a few entrepreneurs were venture-funded based on the fantasy of the many eyeballs their product would generate. Investors often gauged them on their ability to spend. If you wrote a business plan, said some onlookers, you were uncool.

We had just started Mindtree and were still struggling to get our second, third and fourth customers. Amidst this, every now and then, dapper young men would show up and suggest that, for a fee, they could create a 'roll up' of a number of start-ups like ours, which would raise the valuation of Mindtree overnight. Then they would hoist us as the management in charge, help take the combined, puffed-up-like-a-rainforest-frog company public and, in the process, give us the currency to acquire an even larger firm, and become rich and famous.

We stayed away from them and struggled through our infancy with old-fashioned hard work. It was slow and sometimes frustrating, particularly following the end of the telecom bubble, 9/11 and the eventual dot-com collapse. Circumstances required us to change our strategy; we focused on execution, took salary cuts, built systems and processes, and went out to the marketplace to sell. It took us a good eight years from the time we had started the company to acquire the critical mass and self-confidence to list at the stock exchange. In between, the magic peddlers vanished one by one and, when we last heard of them, were all looking for jobs. So you know why? They were fortune hunters and were telling us how we should build a company without ever having done it themselves.

The real credit for helping us stay the course goes to our founder-chairman, Ashok Soota, as much as to our initial investors, Global Technology Venture and Walden International, who remained patiently by our side. Ashok Soota told us early in the game not to get carried away with the valuation talk, but to focus on getting paying customers who would stay with us. In fact, he set out the mandate: go public only when Mindtree has a revenue of $100 million and 100 customers. This took us all the way until 2005 and we waited another two years to make sure our processes would stand the rigours needed to run a listed company. A listed company is required to manage investor expectations and has enormous obligations with regard to regulatory compliance.

Contrast this with what happens to most start-ups. Many get taken in by the magic the 'roll up' guys weave and begin to chase a pipe dream, or get swayed by the very convincing arguments that are put on the table, such as: What if the gravy train never returns?

The chimera of chasing valuations may go further upstream. I have come across many would-be entrepreneurs who have spent money to get a third party to suggest the valuation of an unborn enterprise. Such a certification is never considered by a real investor, who has his own yardstick to measure how much the company may be worth. The valuation of your company, in the end, is not about someone saying how much you are worth, but about who has put money in your bank and what percentage of the company they now own. At the time of inception, the first investor, often called an angel, will bet on the entrepreneur and the business idea and put in a small amount of money so that the company can get off the ground. For this the angel will get a certain percentage of ownership. Once the company gets going, a venture capital firm may step in with what is called a 'first round' of funding that truly reflects the initial valuation of the company. From that point on the company's valuation will come from a combination of real factors. These are, primarily, a differentiated business idea, having paying customers and retaining them, garnering process maturity, determining the leadership pipeline, creating a product roadmap, gaining clarity on investment priorities, ensuring cash flow from the business, good governance and overall reputation. Focusing on these issues requires clarity of vision, and an enormous amount of time and hard work.

Central to this is the risk that an entrepreneur takes. What if all the hard work leads nowhere because the product fails, the competition is merciless, or the market tanks? What if the valuation of the company drops even in the eyes of its current investors? Such risks will always remain, but if an entrepreneur is truly focused the end result cannot but be the creation of something valuable. And if you build something inherently valuable there will always be someone willing to invest in it or buy it.

For a small set of start-ups that are finally ready for public listing, the issue of valuation returns. Merchant bankers, whose fees depend on how much they can inflate your valuation, often mislead you. An entrepreneur needs to be very realistic about what his company's IPO price should be. For the ones that get over-valued, the market is often ruthless. The consequent loss is not just financial; it is a loss of reputation.

After the telecom and dot-com collapse of the 1990s, a

series of economic slowdowns has kept the bubble-makers on a break. At the same time, history tends to repeat itself. From the famous Tulip bubble of the 1600s to the recurring real-estate bubbles in the course of the world's economic history, 'roll up kids' have never really gone away. If someone tells you an absurdly fancy number or shows you a path to double or treble your company's valuation overnight, take a deep breath and remember what you've read here. Life is about constant growth, but any unnatural growth is inherently destructive.

PART III

SCALING YOUR INTELLECT

10

THE WISE MEN AROUND THE TABLE

> 'A board member is not supposed to be a yes-man, a business development manager or, worse still, a fixer. When chosen well and respected, a board is the conscience keeper, and the voice of reason and caution, for leaders willing to listen.'

WHEN WE STARTED MINDTREE, we constituted a board with four founders and provided board seats to three of our early investors. As the company geared up to go public, sometime in 2006, the then founder-chairman, Ashok Soota, started the process of expanding the board with independent directors. We felt that the board needed to be reconstituted with new members well before taking the company public so that the new directors and Mindtree could get up to speed with each other. Among all of us, it was Ashok who had the knowledge, maturity and foresight to put together a stellar board that would not just 'look good' but lead well. The independent directors were chosen for their proven managerial ability, personal leadership qualities, integrity, ability to ask critical questions, diversity and, last but not least, their willingness to devote the time needed to make key contributions to the functioning of the organization.

When people think about an enterprise from the outside, they recognize the entrepreneur or the most senior person in the ranks, some of the top leaders and perhaps the spokespeople, but they don't usually associate a board of directors with it because they neither get to see nor hear the board. (Except, of course, when there is some bad news, like the CEO being fired for non-performance or, worse still, a corporate scandal or regulatory failure.) Leave aside the outsider; often, the people leading an enterprise do not think about the board or attach as much value to it as they should.

A board member is not supposed to be a yes-man, a business development manager or, worse still, a fixer. The board's job is to select the CEO, guide and assist with the development of the long-term strategy of the company, formulate policies and procedures, review financial results, provide good governance and, above all, protect the interests of the smallest shareholder of the company. The crucial starting point for an entrepreneur is, therefore, in the careful selection of the board members, keeping in mind that these individuals will add immensely by way of wisdom, guidance and knowledge, which are essential to the company's growth and ability to scale.

When companies start, they are usually unlisted entities and begin as either proprietary or private limited companies. The concept of a board does not apply to the former, but the latter statutorily requires the formation and regular functioning of a board of directors. Mostly, entrepreneurs and top-level managers consider putting together a board a mere formality and find comfort in one that is not going to question the running of the organization. In most cases board members do not meet formally. Documents are signed by them retrospectively and filed for the benefit of compliance with the law. Entrepreneurs often invite their friends and family to constitute the board, causing the board to lose the arm's length required for functioning without fear or prejudice. In any case these people do not possess the abilities to contribute in the way a board of directors is meant to.

A publicly listed corporation requires the appointment of 'independent directors'. 'Independence' implies that they have no vested interest in or personal transactions with the organization. The spirit behind the idea is that independent directors look out for the interests of the shareholders and the organization ahead of all else in case a choice has to be made at any time between the management's position on a matter and the greater good of the enterprise.

Prior to going public, we got on board several people who met the criteria: Albert Hieronimus, N. Vittal, Mark Runacres, R. Srinivasan, and George Scalise and, later, David Yoffie. Albert was the head of Bosch in India, a man well-versed in European and Indian business practices. N. Vittal had retired as the chief vigilance commissioner of India and prior to that was one of the initiators of the IT revolution in the country. Mark was a research fellow at The Energy and Resources Institute (TERI) and had earlier been a career diplomat with the British Foreign Service. Srinivasan was a well-known industry leader and ex-head of Widia India. George Scalise had been at the helm of the US Semi-Conductor Association. David taught strategy at Harvard Business School and had been a director on Intel's board for over twenty years. Each individual brought great value to the Mindtree board and made it rich. More importantly, they weren't our friends and family.

One important aspect of an effective board is the regularity and intensity of its meetings. Ashok had instituted the discipline in us to publish the dates for board meetings a year ahead so that people coming from overseas could plan their travel. This may seem like a minor issue. Most organizations take it lightly and change dates often, adversely affecting the quality of preparation, attendance and deliberation at the meeting. The internal team at Mindtree prepared and circulated the board docket well in advance so that the directors could read it prior to their arrival. The day-long quarterly huddle was always run with precision. The reading material for each meeting easily ran into a hundred pages and sometimes more. In addition to the quarterly meetings to review results, the board's sub-committees like the strategic initiatives committee, the audit committee, the administrative committee, the compensation committee, the nomination committee and the share-holder grievance committee met separately to study and assess past as well as future issues and the action plan going forward.

It is one thing to have a stellar board; it is quite another to use it effectively. The latter requires the capacity to seek and receive counsel, and tremendous maturity on the part of the management. Above all, it requires intellectual honesty. When Mindtree decided to get into an ill-conceived diversification of designing smartphone technology (mentioned earlier in the chapter titled 'The M&A Myths'), believing it would bring us closer to our goal of becoming a billion-dollar company, we went to the board asking them to approve the acquisition and the subsequent capital infusion we would be making. The board approved the plan. In every subsequent board meeting, we made presentations on what we thought to be reasonable progress even as some of us had started doubting the feasibility of the idea. When a prototype of what we had thought would be a game-changing smartphone was ready, we showed it to the board members and asked them what they thought of it. It never occurred to us that the members had no specific domain expertise and would not be in a position to question the hundreds of gaps in the design and engineering of the gadget. They could at most ask a set of broad questions and raise telltale issues, but expecting them to get into lower-level specifics was serious folly on our part. We had slipped into confirmation bias. What we should have done was hire the best brand and marketing experts, and the smartest Silicon Valley lawyers who knew Intellectual Property laws, approach the finest research institutions that the leading players in the industry consulted, and retain the best engineering consulting firms who alone could tell us that we were babes in the wood. The board nodded its head appreciatively when the prototype of the smartphone was passed around, assuming that we knew what we were doing because, after all, they too had great respect for the management team. The result, as I've described earlier, was a near-death experience for Mindtree. But when the crisis hit, our stellar board rose to the occasion, helped us recover from our mistakes and shepherded us back to base. Had it not been for the wise men around the table, we would have simply gone out of business.

Yet, however great a board may be, it can be misled, sometimes with disastrous outcomes, if the management team is unscrupulous. A great example is what happened in the case of Satyam Computer Services in 2009. At one time, the company was among India's top five software services companies and had broken through the billion-dollar barrier thanks to the entrepreneurial spirit and ambition of its founders and the sheer hard work of close to a hundred thousand employees. It was a family-run company, with wheels within wheels, but to the external world it presented a reasonable picture of professionalism, enough to be listed in the Indian and US stock markets. The founders carefully covered their many small and progressively larger breaches of integrity and acts of poor governance. Finally, they got bold enough to not only try larger fraud but also get the board to approve the acquisition of shady real-estate firms run by the chairman Ramalinga Raju's sons. Satyam had a stellar board but it could not see through the devious management intent behind the acquisitions. Eventually, the company imploded, the Chairman and the CFO went to jail, and the independent board members went on to suffer lifelong professional ignominy.

A board's primary function is to set broad directions, to oversee the management's strategy, sanction resources and ensure governance. It must, therefore, spend substantial time helping the management peer into the future. In its deliberations, the attention it gives to issues future and past should be in the ratio of 70:30. It is extremely important for the management to constantly ask itself, 'What is the board spending its time and energy on? How wisely are we utilizing our advisers?' While the board should certainly scrutinize financial reports every quarter, if that becomes its primary activity then there is a serious problem. It is the job of the management to have a firm handle on the financials for the current quarter and the next few quarters, but they must remember that the board has been engaged to look at the financials, prospects and opportunities for the coming year and the years after that.

The board, when chosen well and respected, is the conscience keeper, and the voice of reason and caution for leaders willing to listen. The board represents wisdom; the management team brings in the intellect and the capacity to execute. Without wisdom, the intellect can only achieve so much and can even be destructive. Crooked management behaviour aside, even well-meaning attempts to scale have seen companies cave in under its own weight. In setting the strategic direction for an organization that wants to scale and prudently questioning the management's capacity to execute, the board becomes the guardian angel that balances the three-legged stool of investor, customer and employee expectations. It is the board's acumen that will ensure that an enterprise appears to the onlooker as the quintessential gliding swan rather than a dog furiously paddling its way across the water.

11

WHEN THE SHEPHERD NEEDS HELP

> ‘When good consultants and good companies team up, unusual new value gets created. But remember, you will invariably get all you need from the consultant in the first six months of engagement. After that, whoever they may be, they are simply repeating themselves.’

THERE ARE AS MANY stories as there are jokes about consultants. One of my favourites is about a shepherd who encounters one while grazing his flock in the countryside. A man appears from nowhere, screeches to a halt, steps out of a fancy automobile and offers to tell the shepherd the exact number of animals he has in his flock if the latter agrees to give him a sheep. The shepherd says, ‘All right.’ The man takes out his smartphone, jabs at a couple of keys, downloads a few industry reports, activates an applet, and within a few minutes tells the shepherd he has 1,628 grazing animals. The shepherd is dumbfounded. The man then points to the animals and asks, ‘Now can I pick up one of the sheep?' The shepherd nods. The man picks out an animal, puts it in the car and is ready to zoom off when the shepherd says, 'Hey, wait a minute. If I tell you your profession, will you give my animal back?' 'Okay,' says the man with a smirk. 'You are a consultant,' the shepherd announces. This time, it is the consultant's jaw that drops. 'How on earth could you tell?' he asks in complete astonishment. The shepherd says, 'Well, first you stopped by without an invitation. Second, you know nothing about the subject on which you offered expert advice. And third, the animal in your car isn't a sheep. It's my dog.'

Despite the disdain in the joke towards consultants, there can be no doubt that when good consultants and good companies team up, unusual new value gets created. All the knowledge and skills needed for an organization to scale are not always available within it. Identifying these areas and looking for the required capabilities to be brought in from outside is one of the key steps to achieving significant and sustained growth. Good consultants can boost the existing intellectual capacity of an organization. They bring in the best practices of leading players in the industry. They question the status quo, help introduce newer ways of doing things, and move on after their job is done.

However, not all organizations know how to engage with consultants.

Working in Wipro with the company's chairman Azim Premji taught me some truly valuable lessons on dealing effectively with consultants – lessons I have implemented and built upon in the years after. Here are some of them.

Lesson #1: Before approaching a consultant and signing them on, speak to the consultant's other clients. The principle behind doing a reference check while hiring someone senior applies here too. Ask a set of well-thought-out questions. Enquire about the process the client followed to choose the consultant. Ask about the way they went about engaging with each other, the various phases of the engagement. Find out carefully about the highs and lows of the engagement process, and what the essentials were in achieving the desired outcome. Some of the other points to cover are: What was the total outlay for the project? How much should one budget for engagement overruns? Once in, does the consultant keep expanding the size of his team and needlessly prolong the engagement? During the conversation, don't hesitate to ask whatever you want – it is up to the clients to share details with you. A client who has had a good experience will invariably be forthcoming with the relevant information and such knowledge will prove invaluable for you before you get started.

Lesson #2: Always be clear about what you are expecting from a consultant and what their expectations are from you as their client. Ask your consulting partner what will make you an ideal client for them and settle the team that will work on your account. The first question makes the consultant think about the service they are about to provide and to state their expectations upfront. The second ensures that you do not get impressed with the presentation given by a partner in the firm only to realize later that most of the actual work will be done by a greenhorn in their set-up who may have theoretical knowledge galore but does not possess the ability to push the envelope. However great a consultant may be, it is essential to ask for a formal project plan and periodically review its progress.

Before any large staff meeting with a consultant it helps to have a short, closed-door conversation on the issues at hand and how the engagement is going to be steered. Many entrepreneurs and CEOs hire consultants and then make two common mistakes: they speak for much of the time trying to impress the consultant and end up stage-managing the subsequent show. They forget that the consultant is not their stooge and is certainly not being paid to hear the CEO's voice!

Lesson #3: A common area of future discomfort while dealing with a consultant has to do with a vague fee structure and payment terms. It is always a good idea to settle the fees and terms of payment ahead of engaging them. Some consultants like to fly business class, be chauffeured (even though the car will idle all day) and stay in 5-star hotels. It is best to set their expectations right about this at the time of settling the engagement. Good consultants respect a frugal company (though matters of hygiene certainly cannot be overlooked!).

There are consultants who will tell you about 'outcome-based pricing'. That is, you pay them a percentage of your net profit or some part of what you gain from improving your manufacturing process, or reducing the number of days of sales outstanding, or something else they may have recommended. It may sound tempting, but there are horror stories that both clients and consultants can share about why such an arrangement did not continue happily ever after. Besides, the pricing or payment terms cannot determine whether or not you will hire someone. Your decision to engage with a consultant cannot be determined by the fact that the person has offered not to charge you upfront. Keep in mind that the reason for your engaging with a consultant is that you believe you need advice to solve a problem and this individual or group has credible evidence of competence in solving it.

Lesson #4: When you hire a consultant, always keep in mind that if you decide to implement his recommendations, you will need to spend at least the same amount of money as the fee you pay them, if not more. When you engage a consultant, you are not obligated to go along with them on everything they recommend. After all, it is your business – not theirs. Reason out their recommendations, push back, argue and ask for evidence. Remember, it is *your* money that will go into implementing the consultant's suggestions.

And, here is the gem: you will invariably get all you need from the consultant in the first six months of engagement. After that, whoever they may be, they are simply repeating themselves.

Lesson #5: Your consultant is not your date. Do not feel bad if the relationship turns out to be incompatible. Whenever you are looking at a long-term engagement, it is a good idea to factor in such a contingency and to set down clear terms on ending the association. Always pay up as per your commitments, and don't speak ill of your erstwhile partners after parting ways. After all, who made the decision to engage with them in the first place?

Lesson #6: In certain cases, there might arise the need for a team of people to work on your project. If a consultant brings along a retinue, you are fully within your rights to examine their individual credentials, offer different levels of fees based on their roles (you cannot pay the make-up artist the same money you pay the star), and periodically assess the value they are adding. Once, while working on a project, Premji realized that an outstanding consultant had brought along a young lady who was adding no value to the meetings or working sessions and performing no other function than being a note-taker at best. Premji called the consultant aside at the end of the day and politely told him to take her off the assignment, or at least not have Wipro paying for her airfare and hotel stay. The consultant tried to justify why she was needed and how she would add value as the work progressed, but realized quickly enough that Premji was not going to foot her bill. Eventually she was taken off the job without loss of goodwill on either side.

Lesson #7: If a consultant is being hired to implement something that must be replicated in multiple other places within your organization, you should ensure that the knowledge is transferred in-house. Put together some of your best operating people and a few from your learning organization and build an in-house team. Let them be a part of the initial study, the recommendation process and the change management that accompanies the typical roll-out. You will be surprised how, after the first one or two roll-outs, the in-house team will easily take on the subsequent ones. This, too, can be settled upfront with the consultant; many of them have train-the-trainer arrangements for a fee or can bundle it as a part of the deal.

Lesson #8: Very often people build unrealistic expectations around consulting engagements without first demonstrating their personal willingness to change. For example, if you are not going to change the poor quality of your raw material, then engaging a Six Sigma or Lean consultant is a waste. When an organization calls in a consultant for an area like strategy, structure, brand or operational efficiency, the most common internal response is a cynical, 'Oh, here's another flavour of the season.' Such scepticism is justified because of the sheer number of initiatives that clueless companies adopt hoping that they will somehow be propelled forward by using them. A business leader must, therefore, appreciate the reason for such cynicism and personally establish the purpose of the engagement to the organization by demonstrating commitment through investing time at the conceptualization, roll-out and review stages.

There is a famous story about how Henry Ford learnt his lesson in demonstrating personal commitment. Ford hired the quality management guru Edward Deming to train his people on quality principles. In the kick-off meeting, he introduced Deming, spoke briefly about the critical need for quality management and then, leaving Deming to do the rest, left the room. As he was walking out, he realized Deming was following him. Surprised, he asked what had happened. In answer, Deming famously quipped that he was simply following the leader. Ford immediately realized his mistake and turned back to sit down with his team to learn about Total Quality Management (TQM).

With Premji there were no such issues. When Wipro initiated Six Sigma, I scouted around the world to find a consulting firm that could guide the organization in its undertaking of the TQM journey. We chose to work with Motorola University. Motorola had embraced TQM and gone on to win the Malcolm Baldridge National Quality Award for performance excellence. Subsequently, Motorola set up a consulting group called Motorola University to help other companies embrace TQM. The engagement started with a week-long training for the top management and Premji was present for the entire duration with all the business unit heads and their reports. Six Sigma principles entail near-zero defect in quality and the process asks leaders to embrace the idea of quality in a personal way. Premji led the way with a personal quality project. He considered meetings as his product or service, and participants in the meetings as his customers. At the end of every meeting, Premji started giving out feedback forms that rated the quality of the meeting on various parameters. The forms were returned to 'Mission: Quality', where we analysed them and went back to Premji on the defect levels of the meetings and a root-cause analysis so that his meetings could be 'measured, analysed, controlled and improved' as per the principles of TQM. The exercise excited curiosity and drew chuckles in the beginning but soon the entire organization got the message that at Wipro quality was taken extremely seriously and could never be compromised on in any area of work.

Lesson #9: It is not unusual for organizations engaging a McKinsey or a Bain or a BCG to be in awe of the super-smart consultants. It is important to respect the consultant. If he does not evoke respect, why have you hired him in the first place? But respect is one thing; awe is another. Being in awe of a consultant makes for a dysfunctional relationship. The most profound knowledge of a consultant still needs the hands of an entrepreneur or a practising manager to create something of value out of it.

PART IV

SCALING YOUR REPUTATION

12

A BRAND NEW YOU

> A brand literally takes birth, grows and ages and, unless it is renewed, it dies and decays. The brand is an expression of an organization's mission, vision, values, its reputation and ambition, and it cannot change unless the core goes through a transformation first.

IN THE FIRST DECADE of our journey the Mindtree brand and its logo served us well. We went about defining the brand in a systematic manner, starting with articulating the DNA of the organization: Imagination, Action and Joy. Then we settled the organization's mission and vision. At that stage we commissioned a name search and, using professional help, settled for MindTree (after the rebranding in 2012, this was changed to Mindtree). At that point, in search of a visual identity for the organization, we went to a school for children with cerebral palsy and conducted a weeklong workshop to explain the idea of the new company. The children then created several logos out of which we chose one that was to become our visual identity for the first phase of our journey. The school was put on Mindtree's stock option plan, and the story of how the Mindtree logo was created became widely known.

When we introduced Mindtree to new customers, we started by presenting the company's DNA, its mission, vision and values, and spoke about our visual identity. To prospective buyers we positioned Mindtree as the best mid-size IT services provider. When pitching to the CIO of a Fortune 500 company, we spoke about the importance of a twin vendor strategy. 'You need the big provider all right, but to de-risk putting all the eggs in the same basket, you need a second vendor. That second vendor should be a mid-size company,' was our key message. Because of our size and keenness to deliver we said that we would be able to bring greater attention, agility and access than larger companies in the business. The message was received well. Over the years, the company evolved with distinctive characteristics: we were an inclusive, warm, employee- and customer-focused organization. When people spoke about us, they said we were unique among the companies they knew in our space. When prodded to define what they meant by 'different', they invariably alluded to our culture. There was no doubt in anyone's mind that Mindtree's culture was unique, it was the essence of the Mindtree brand. This was a great thing, except that in the second phase of our growth it just wasn't enough.

We were by then solidly entrenched in specific verticals and had built large, complex solutions for some of our customers, but our messaging was clearly falling short. Imagine you are the CIO of a Fortune 500 company and a sales guy tells you a compulsive story that tugs at your heart. You may quite like it and give him some business, but if your mind is preoccupied with a heavy-lifting, enterprise-wide transformational IT project that entails an outlay of $50 million or $100 million or $200 million and on which your professional reputation rests, you will be looking for competence in your area of requirement (in this case, domain knowledge, technological depth and ability to lead the client) rather than the culture that sets a service apart. In large IT deals the client requires its associate companies to go beyond being 'order takers' to becoming 'order makers'. They can no longer wait for the client to ask them to do something. Instead, they must imagine a solution, take the idea to the client, think through the implementation issues and lead the way. Further, when a company acquires a certain size and looks at greater future growth, it must enter into the consideration set of newer customers. These customers must view the company as capable of putting forth fresh business models and innovative products, and serving wider markets. As

Mindtree worked harder to broaden its customer base and get in big business with its original pitch, the CIOs we approached did not see these crucial messages jumping out. Not in our sales pitch, not in our collaterals, not on our website. It was clear that before we got around to scaling our business, our brand needed a serious re-vision.

I learnt the essentials of branding from a rather colourful man named Shombit Sengupta who founded Shining Strategic Design, a brand advisory in Paris. When I first met him around 1996, his company had a reported turnover of $9 million, his brands sold for over $40 billion worldwide for companies like Danone of France and Lakme in India. Legend had it that if you went into any kitchen in Europe, you would see at least six products that carried his signature.

Shombit taught me that a brand is not just a logo, a tagline or a smart-sounding name. It is the perception of the value of a company, product or service in the mind of a customer, and perception is partly rational and partly emotional. The process of brand building, then, is the externalization of the inner value of a corporation, product or service. When you consider a brand, it is not something that only touches a paying customer. A brand has many stakeholders, and chief among them are the employees of the company. For them, brand association leads to pride in the company, often referred to as 'badge value'. The other key aspect of the employee–brand connect is that the employee is a personification of the brand value of the company. Take the FedEx employee who delivers a package, for instance, or the Singapore Airline air hostess, or the McKinsey consultant.

Whether it belongs to a product or a service or a corporation, the brand lives in a dynamic, ever-changing world. Thus the perception of specific values a brand evokes is relative. A brand literally takes birth, grows and ages and, unless it is renewed, it dies and decays. In the hyper-competitive, global markets of today, the time between the birth and the decay of a brand is continuously shrinking. A company that wants to remain fresh and appealing must rethink its brand at periodic intervals. And because the brand is an expression of the company's mission, vision, values, its reputation and ambition, it cannot change unless the core goes through a transformation first.

In 2011, a decade after the successful launch of Mindtree and the subsequent evolution of its brand, we realized that our future lay in winning large deals. This meant that we had to deliver a new brand promise beyond being seen as nice guys. Our future depended on establishing that we are expertise-led and culture-backed; not the other way around. For this crucial exercise we decided to seek external help.

After assessing the credentials of four major brand advisories around the world and then looking at the mutual fit (not all great agencies are meant for you), we settled for Siegel+Gale based in New York. They had created the brand identity, logos and other visual elements for companies like Dell, Southwest Airlines, parts of Microsoft and SAP. Remember the slanted 'E' in Dell, which was meant to symbolize Michael Dell's wish to 'turn the world on its ear'? That was their idea. They are the people who made Southwest Airlines's brand identity one of the most admired in the US. What we liked about them was their empathy for 'challenger' brands, or brands that might not have all the credentials of the present market leaders in their segment but are ready to question the status quo and eat into the market share of existing, larger competitors. Dell did that with larger computer companies like IBM, and Southwest did it with bigger players in the airlines sector like Delta and American Airlines.

Many organizations do not realize that a brand advisory is not an ad agency. The former researches your current brand, helps you discover the aspirational brand values and reposition your brand. An ad agency takes over where a brand advisory signs off by communicating the brand through several channels and ensuring that a unified message in presented across these channels.

When you settle for a brand advisory, the starting point is the assimilation of the core team that will run with your project at their end. An involved re-branding exercise takes close to a year from the start to the rolling-out phase, so it is very important to build trust and confidence in the team that will work on your project. In the beginning, a lot of care must be taken to ensure that the team gets to fully understand your business, competitive environment, core issues, challenges and everything else that you would tell someone joining you at a very senior level in the company. At the same time, an internal brand council needs to be set up to work closely with the brand advisory. Who you choose as members of the council has a great bearing on the exercise. They must be people who have credibility as leaders, and can influence the adoption of not just a new brand identity but potentially new organizational values and fresh ways of working. In short, your brand council should consist of change managers.

After the assimilation phase, the brand advisory, with the help of and overseen by the brand council, will typically do some preliminary research on the gap between where the company is with its present brand and where it wants to go. With this knowledge in place, it will move on to in-depth research into the two key stakeholders: the employees of the company, who live the brand, and the customers and clients who buy its products and services. When we did the exercise, 2000 of our employees were asked to poll and hundreds of customers at various levels in their respective organizations were interviewed. The results were eye-opening.

By 2011, most of the leaders at Mindtree who now

represented the company were all folks who came on board during our initial days as a start-up. Naturally, they had a certain set of expectations from the organization. The rest of the employees were mostly from the current generation, now commonly termed as Gen-Y, and cared little about a value system that was as old as the company. Imagine a 22-year-old working in Mindtree in 2011. In 1999, when we started, the individual was 10 years old and would feel no connect whatsoever with our pitch.

The findings from the customer research were even more telling. Our customers saw us as 'nice', 'humble' and 'introspective'. This was good to hear but if we were to be called to the table for large, transformative deals, then we would need CIOs to perceive us as strategic, bold and decisive. Our present brand identity wasn't going to cut it. We needed to convey the voice of the brand differently. That voice had to be bold, confident and active in all forms of communication, be it in a slide deck, in the look and feel and content of our website, our intranet, the corporate presentation and collaterals, a video film or the annual report. More importantly, to change the brand perception we would need to move over from the mission, vision and organizational values we had created in 1999.

The extensive exercise that followed led us to adopt a new mission statement that more appropriately described the kind of company we wanted to be. The new values that were introduced were whittled down to three from an existing set of five. We wanted Mindtree to stand for 'Collaborative Spirit, Unrelenting Dedication and Expert-Thinking', to be projected as capable of building a billion-dollar, domain-focused company that would be respected for its work.

The old logo had tugged at the hearts of many, but we realized that it tugged at the hearts of people only when they were told the story. But at a trade show where the logo stands shoulder to shoulder on a standee with those of Accenture, IBM and TCS, there is no one to tell the story. The bigger problem was that while the logo was a work of art, it completely overwhelmed the name of the company. Thus, our target audience, customers in US, UK and Europe, did not register the name of the company that owned the logo and did not associate any value with it. The logo had to change. For the first time, along with the new logo, Mindtree adopted a tagline: 'Welcome to Possible'.

With a new positioning as an expertise-led and culture-backed company, we now had a new set of values. These reflected in the way the new brand presented itself in every aspect of communication – from our stationery to internal merchandising, from the design of our physical workspace to our website, everything was changed. All in all, our people and our customers got the message: We were no longer the old MindTree. We were now on the path to building a newer, more relevant Mindtree, a company that would make businesses and societies flourish.

The brand journey is unique to every organization. No two are going to be alike. The Mindtree story I've related here serves to show how involved that process is, how much attention it requires from the top management, and how it must be seen as a strategic, organization-wide exercise in transformation. Only then can it unlock a company's potential and build new value, both critical factors in building scale.

13

THE FOURTH ESTATE

> ‘When it comes to dealing with the media, being authentic is a virtue.’

IT IS SAID THAT for any company a square centimetre of news coverage is worth ten times more than paid advertising. When a company is born it attracts a lot of interest, as with a baby. The media likes start-up stories, because they are all about the spirit of entrepreneurship and innovation and are always quite charming. As an organization grows and navigates through its juvenile days, the charm slowly fades and somewhere down the line it ceases to evoke media interest. Very few organizations understand the power of the media and work on it in a planned, cohesive and wise manner. When dealt with intelligently, beyond the quips and quotable quotes, the media can significantly scale a company's reputation.

I used to think that speaking to the press or appearing on the television required no special knowledge or training. You need to know what you are talking about, and be smart and eloquent. I also thought that the key to favourable media relations was essentially to be available, friendly and interesting. That completely changed when Mindtree started its operations and I went to the US. There I realized how important it is to know how to deal with the print and the television world. I learned from public relations experts how to listen to a question, how speaking to a print journalist was different from speaking on camera, the meaning of messaging, and a host of other dos and don'ts.

When I returned to India I realized a sea change had taken place within a matter of a few years. Print and electronic media had burgeoned and there was a new level of professionalism and sophistication that was now in place. I thanked my stars that I had received formal training in media interaction and could now interact with the media beyond being friendly and interesting.

The basic requirement is to understand what the media really wants, and to keep in mind that the media is primarily looking for news, opinion and thought leadership. Let us look at these in a little more detail.

Newspapers, magazines and television channels are perennially hungry for news, but simply feeding the media with what an organization considers news will have no result. News of a product launch or breakthrough research, of beating the analyst's forecast of the results for the quarter or the opening of a new office will make newspeople yawn. You need to know what is really newsworthy and then be judicious about doling it out. Look at the information you want to convey from the media's point of view. Why should they carry the story? What is special or unique about it? The questions may kill undue temptation, and may also help you to refine your communication to the media and present the matter in a way that serves a bigger purpose. For instance, a company may want to hire 10,000 people in the year to come. While the fact may not be newsworthy in itself, its tenor changes when it involves the company making a foray into tier-II cities to hire people, or going the extra mile to take on women candidates in higher numbers, or recruiting people with disabilities. Similarly, a new drug formulation may not be big news but the fact that a team of researchers well under the age of 30 has achieved it may be extremely newsworthy.

The media is not always about news. It is also about opinion. If the leader of an organization is seen as an expert and known to have credibility, the media often seeks him out for an opinion. What do you think of so-and-so making such-and-such announcement? What do you think should be the priority for the newly elected government? What are your thoughts on the garbage problem the city is facing? What do you have to say about some highly placed official or an industry stalwart who has made a gender-insensitive comment? What is your take on political reforms and corruption? Do you think Party A or Party B should come to power? It can be on any topic that is news for the day.

Being quoted frequently can mean that the leader is visible, that he is someone whose opinion is of value – and this may rub off on his organization and its image. However, problems may arise. By frequently commenting on issues unrelated to his business the person may become a talking head, and speaking on everything under the sun may diffuse his image and that of his organization. Just as an internal assessment of newsworthiness of the information about to be put out gives it credibility, sharing an opinion on a matter not directly related to the organization is best done in small measures and with a specific purpose. When it comes to dealing with the media, being authentic is a virtue. The ability to deflect (by saying something like, 'I am not the authority on it, why don't I connect you to someone else I know?') and sometimes even saying a polite but firm 'No' go a long way in building respect and gaining reliability with the media.

Whether it is releasing news, commenting on an issue or the dissemination of thought leadership, working with the media must be seen as a matter of organizational strategy. It helps to train senior leaders to appreciate how the media works and what they must and must not do while engaging with it. The starting point for this is to engage a competent and professional public relations agency that can help an organization with its long-term communication and, as part of that, the media strategy. A good agency can bring great value, not as a mere executor but as an advisor, particularly in times of difficulty, such as an adverse report appearing in the press.

Of equal import is paying attention to each interaction with the media. An individual who has been asked for an interview should start by researching the journalist well in advance, and determining his goals and expectations. Even if the two happen to know each other at a personal level, it is crucial to treat the journalist as a professional, and deal with him or her respectfully and with preparedness.

In today's always-on world, a simple Google search can give access to the last three stories filed by a media person. Reading them will give the individual a good sense of the potential treatment of a story in the journalist's hands. However short the interaction may be, failing to prepare for it is dangerous. The individual might think the journalist wants to research a story on the company or on him as a successful leader, but the interest may be founded in serious doubts about the business, or some ill-founded rumour about how it is being conducted.

Being friendly, cooperative and approachable with the media will always lend an advantage, but it becomes a problem when an organization is saddled with bad news. The media will be relentless in getting to the heart of the story and having courted them actively in the past, a spokesperson or leader might find himself in a catch-22 situation. He may not have anything to hide but may be prohibited from making a public statement because of a regulatory issue or a possible fallout of the news that could have serious repercussions for the business. Silence may lead to wrong or damaging conclusions being drawn by the press or others. If you are caught in such a situation, don't panic. (If this hasn't happened already, your business probably hasn't grown up yet!) You are not under compulsion to respond immediately and have the right to ask for time. Reach out to your PR firm, and senior colleagues, sometimes even your board and, if the need arises, speak to your lawyer for counsel.

There may be an occasion when a newspaper carries an unreasonable story about you. It may contain incorrect details and erroneous conclusions, and sometimes these may be potentially damaging. You can send out a denial or a letter to refute the story and they may even publish it, but chances are that it will be carried in an obscure corner of the paper or magazine that readers will fail to notice. The better and more lasting recourse is to visit the newspaper office and have a respectful but firm conversation. For such a meeting, be prepared with facts and involve as little emotion as possible.

Despite how well you manage your media relations, there

may come a time when unintended damage is caused because of a faux pas or an error of judgement. Here is the most glorious gaffe from my closet.

There are a few journalists for whom I have tremendous respect. One of them happens to be Pankaj Mishra. At the time, he had just moved to the financial newspaper *Mint* and invited me to a conversation for their weekend supplement, *Lounge*. The discussion was about entrepreneurship and related matters. It was quite flattering because Pankaj said that he wanted me to speak to him as a thought leader.

We met, and the conversation took many interesting twists and turns until we came to the subject of contrasting entrepreneurs with successful managers. Pankaj wanted to know why most successful managers, great professionals themselves, do not start their own ventures. I responded by saying that start-up entrepreneurs must do with a lot less, deal with uncertainty and rejection, and must have great survival skills. They are more like mongrels; nothing is guaranteed for them. They must forage, fight and run for cover when danger arrives in the shape of the municipal dog-catcher. Then, instead of stopping there, I went on to contrast the mongrel with pedigree dogs that enjoy comfort, security and safety, though all of it comes with a collar around the neck. Many highly placed professionals are like pedigree dogs, I said.

A couple of days later, a full-page interview appeared in every regional edition of *Mint*, complete with a couple of flattering photographs. The headline read: 'Successful Executives are Like Pedigree Dogs: Mindtree's Bagchi'. I could not have imagined in my wildest dreams that a sentence like that could have become a headline for the interview I had given. Taken out of context my words meant something totally different from what I had intended. We had spoken on many subjects for over an hour and a half and any of the interesting, colourful sentences I had spoken could have made for a suitable headline. Why did it have to be this one, I wondered. Even as many people found the interview very insightful, for countless others who did not speak up the headline must have seemed brash and in bad taste. I felt miserable, but the fact was that I had said what I had said.

The lesson is simple. In print, when a sentence you have spoken appears as a headline or a quote, its meaning and impact may change beyond your imagination. Someone has said that if a picture is worth a thousand words, a metaphor is worth a thousand pictures. This was one instance when I wish it wasn't the case!

14

THE FORCE OF GOOD

> "CSR initiatives don't just make businesses credible. They have greater benefits. They awaken the power of inclusion and volunteerism among employees, which rub off on the way they approach their work."

ON THE THIRD SATURDAY of every month, a bus leaves Mindtree's office in Bengaluru in the morning, picking up volunteers from designated points in the city. It makes three stops: one at a children's home, another at a home for the destitute and, finally, at a centre for patients suffering from HIV/AIDS. The three homes are run by the Missionaries of Charity. The objective of the occupants of the bus is to give the Charity's sisters a few hours' break from their routine. They carry food and help clean up the place. Sometimes they give the inmates a haircut, or play music for them, and sometimes they take along small items like bangles and trinkets and new clothes. For these software engineers, it is not about doing good. It is about being good. When we thought of starting Mindtree, we had envisioned a company with a social conscience. The monthly bus trip and a dozen other activities that we engage in around the world are a part of this idea. Voluntary work with schools, civic bodies and not-for-profit organizations keeps us connected with larger social issues beyond the everyday lives at the workplace.

In post-independence India, corporate social responsibility (CSR) was an amalgam of what industrialists like Ghanshyam Das Birla, Jamsetji Tata, Lala Shri Ram, Gujarmal Modi and others like them typified. They built temples, dharamshalas and educational institutions, sponsored artists and music festivals. Some got into active community development with specific focus on areas like adult education and family planning, like the well-known Tata initiatives in Jharkhand's tribal belts. Most such work that was traditionally done in India had distinct characteristics. First, such activities did not flow from an overall, articulated corporate mission that bound everyone in the organization. Usually, CSR was about what the owner engaged with and seldom galvanized the collective power of people to make a larger social impact or gave employees an opportunity to view the workplace as a unit of society. Second, the Indian model had little to do with governance. For example, a company could be getting raided for income tax or excise duty evasion and at the same time be known for building dharamshalas as a contribution to society. Third, the concept of CSR had an angle of 'charity' as against building an organizational culture of volunteerism. Finally, CSR as a concept had nothing to do with the organization's philosophy towards its customers. A company in a protected economy could be building schools and colleges but continue to create poor products and services because the customer had no choice but to buy it. An automobile company, for instance, could be doing great charity work while its products continue to not meet emission standards.

Today, CSR has come to mean something else entirely and it is imperative for organizations to adopt it.

Many companies the world over have made CSR a part of their mission, vision and values. They involve people at all levels and have an organizational view of social responsibility. For instance, Toyota set up their green car initiative in the 1990s when the law did not require them to control emissions. Around the same time, reprographic companies like Fuji Xerox had in place clear R&D initiatives to create environment-friendly, green copiers. Lufthansa employees contribute time and money to support the less privileged in all the developing countries where the airline operates. Such initiatives have emanated from within these companies and have a long-term perspective. They are born out of genuine concern and commitment to a larger social need.

In India, we see quite a contrast in awareness and attitude to the larger society. Here, it is okay for me to allow my factories to discharge chemical effluents into a river or the ground until the Supreme Court tells me not to. Industries do not think for themselves about their responsibility towards the environment in which they operate. Let me illustrate the issue with a personal example. For many months, a few of my neighbours were littering the road across my house by dumping garbage on the street. During weekends, I started picking up the randomly dumped garbage to transfer to the dustbin. More than anything else, the process turned out to be a fantastic learning opportunity for me. When you shift garbage, you get to know about consumption patterns of the community just as much as you discover information about packaging and their disposal. Thus, while sifting through the garbage, I found that most of it was made up of plastic and polythene-based food packaging material, and diapers. None of the packaging material or diapers carried any disposal instructions from the big business houses that manufactured and sold these products.

During my childhood, packaging material was reusable, like the tin of Vanaspati ghee that served as a storage container in the kitchen. Biscuits were packaged in paper that was biodegradable. Today, the packaging revolution has meant that plastic and polythene wrappers coated with toxic inks are used to hook the customer from the store shelf. As long as a product outsells its competitors, its manufacturing company does not care how the packaging is disposed of after use. In 2000, I happened to visit the office of a major fast-moving consumer goods (FMCG) company that sells hot and cold beverages. It had vending machines on its premises, equipped with disposable plastic cups of the variety that litters our roads and dust bins and eventually chokes the sewage system. This was a company that had some of the best-educated people in the country at its helm. Why did they not think of using paper cups? There are similar instances everywhere. Corporations in India do not see the link between the products and services they create from the wider angle of CSR. For them CSR is a donation paid for a worthy cause and has nothing to do with their core business.

The good news is that this is beginning to change. There are companies that are beginning to think of the social and environmental consequences of their enterprise, without having to be policed or pushed by the law. These companies believe they must do what is right in a larger social context.

Taken seriously, CSR initiatives make businesses credible. They equally help to bring in a certain quality of customers and attract business alliances that identify with a common cause. People flock to Starbucks because the company actively promotes the Rainforest Alliance, and advocates fair trade and sustainable farming. The followers of Starbucks are emotionally invested in concerns of the planet. But CSR initiatives also have a great impact on people within an organization. Commitment to CSR activities can change the DNA of the organization by awakening the power of inclusion and volunteerism among employees, which rub off on the way they approach their work. They build a higher sense of purpose, see themselves as agents of change, take charge of their tasks and environment, and in some cases even drop the passivity that has so far caused them to view a working day as two swipes and a lunch. At the same time, volunteerism connects them to like-minded people.

■

While most organizations are becoming increasingly aware of the business benefits of CSR, many among them do not know where to start or how to ensure that such activities become a product of conscious-thinking as with any other key business process. Here are some guidelines.

Choose an activity that is close to the heart of the corporation, something that not only excites the CEO but appeals to people at every level. When that happens, people are willing to get involved and want to contribute their time and money. It becomes an important element of their pride in the organization.

Stay with one idea to begin with, take it to a mature level, build critical mass in terms of contribution and employee engagement. After this, look at related issues that your activities can extend to. For instance, truck manufacturers could start with providing better safety equipment and comfort in the driver's cabin, extend that to clean washrooms and showers at trucking points, and then look at the connection between truck drivers and the spread of HIV/AIDS.

Not everyone needs to get involved with primary education and drinking water. The overlap between the zone of concern and zone of impact may be where the business interests of the company lie. A mining company has to make afforestation central to its CSR. A drug company must support wellness. A construction company needs to look at issues surrounding migrant labourers and their families. Such areas cannot be overlooked while a company engages with issues many times removed from it. Sheer proximity gives the leaders and employees of the company special insight into these issues and immediate capability to make an impact.

The spirit of CSR requires sustained engagement with a cause. When it gets reduced to simply writing a cheque or attending a charity function, it falls short of the idea that a business organization can be a force of good. Yet, the world has countless problems, from child abuse to corruption, disability to gender issues, illiteracy to global warming. Business organizations have limited resources, both financially and in terms of management bandwidth to make a positive impact on all the issues that plague humanity. The core competence of a business organization is not social change; they are not a substitute for government, civil society or the not-for-profit sector. With this limitation in mind, once a cause has been identified, the need may arise to join hands with not-for-profit organizations that work in the chosen area.

Choosing one is not simple. Although there is a proliferation of such organizations out there, many of them are ill-managed and have poor standards of governance. Most not-for-profit companies see clean book-keeping as a drag and, as a result, despite good intent, lose track of finances. They are also just as susceptible to governance gaps as businesses are. Therefore, before engaging with a not-for-profit partner, an enterprise must do the same due diligence that precedes its entering a new business area or selecting a strategic supplier. The same rules apply here. Hard questions need to be asked (Who are the people involved in running the organization? What is its track record in the specialized field?), reference checks need to be done, accounting standards and practices asked for, and cultural fit to be determined. Then comes the time to engage.

Working closely with a well-chosen not-for-profit partner has a valuable influence. The not-for-profit sector, by the very nature of its charter, does several things well. They work with larger-than-life problems, build resilience, create alliances, work with frugal resources and, above all, innovate. These are extremely important management capabilities that leaders in business organizations desire in their people. As a business engages with a CSR partner, its own leadership capacity expands and, quite often, its approach to solving business issues becomes very different. These qualities have a subtle characteristic: once they seep in, they stay.

Businesses cannot succeed if society fails. Profitability cannot be sustained if it runs contrary to the larger needs of the social fabric. These are well-articulated postulates. At a simpler level, in each one of us is an innate desire to stay connected with the large world and to contribute to it. An organization is an excellent platform for aggregating the spirit of inclusion and contribution. In the process, it can create a surge of positive energy in the individual employee and multiply it manifold because it has the power of the collective. At the end of the day, good people alone can build good organizations and good societies.

PART V

SCALING YOUR PEOPLE

15

HIRE RIGHT, FIRE RIGHT

> 'When in doubt, don't hire. And when the situation demands it, fire without trembling. In business, it isn't a good idea to be afraid.'

AT MINDTREE, THROUGH SOME hard work and what must have been beginner's luck, we had started building up an impressive portfolio of projects featuring companies like Volvo and Unilever. Encouraged by our initial success, we felt that Mindtree should start looking at itself as a company focused on vertical domains rather than as a generic provider of IT services. Manufacturing could well be where we could start, we told ourselves. Building domain capability in a given vertical requires long-term commitment, investment and leadership. We knew we could bring to the table the first two but were also aware that none of us in the company had a solid manufacturing background or deep software expertise in a related field that we could rely on to establish and raise a manufacturing vertical. This meant we had to get the right person from outside.

At that time it wasn't difficult to zero in on a couple of competitors who had large manufacturing practices. We engaged a search agency. After some looking around, they found a person who headed a 500-people unit solely focused on serving clients in the manufacturing industry vertical of a large company and was willing to consider an offer from us (at the time Mindtree itself employed just a thousand people). The man had great academic credentials and years of experience with his present employer. During the subsequent discussions, a few things worked out rather well for us. He was looking for a change because he was getting bored after spending decades with his present employer. In addition, we were a high-profile, pre-IPO start-up and could provide the freedom and flexibility for him to build something ground up. The deal was done, he came on board and we got off to a hopeful start.

However, things did not go quite the way either we or the person had imagined. To begin with, he experienced disappointments on arrival and, as happens in such cases, these remained bottled up. At the time of interviewing him we had not mentioned that we had a largely open office, that there were no personal assistants and the overall atmosphere was entrepreneurial, frugal, bootstrap. He was leaving behind decades of experience in a structured, large organization where the ethos was different. There, he had had support systems in place – from personal assistants to systems and procedures – and lifelines all around. There were downloadable forms and automatic request handlers. You could simply type in a search and instantly get whitepapers, point-of-view documents, PowerPoint slides, and analyst reports on subscription from the Gartners and the IDGs of the world. In other words, you were accessorized. Mindtree's set-up, like any start-up's, was ragtag. If you needed a whitepaper or a slide deck on a subject, you burnt the midnight oil and created your own. We didn't have subscriptions to analyst reports. If you had the money, you used it to buy an air ticket to make a sales call, not to buy analyst reports.

Despite the stark differences between his previous company and Mindtree, he trudged along. But as time went by frustration started to build up on our side. As far as he was concerned, he was there to guide, manage and direct; we wanted him to be the doer. We had thought of the manufacturing vertical as a start-up within a start-up and to make that happen he needed to bring in business. If he could not lead us to or help close new business, where would we get the vertical capability? There is a stark difference between a subject-matter expert and someone who can get a vertical off the ground. We had assumed that a highly knowledgeable person like him would use his strategic thinking, contacts and business savvy to bring in big business.

Unfortunately, people with his kind of knowledge don't always think like businessmen. The mistake we had made was clear, and even though both sides tried their best we eventually had to part ways.

When an organization wants to reach the next orbit it will always look for people who can help it to scale. But working towards scale and a prior experience of functioning in an already scaled environment are not the same thing. From that one failed experience at Mindtree I learnt something very valuable: when you're hiring for a fresh phase of growth, don't hire for education, years of experience or pedigree. Hire for the candidate's ability to build, his capacity to think differently, and ensure that you're not hiring someone who cannot think beyond the success formula of his previous organization. That is like raising a tiger cub in a cat's womb.

It is said that even after an entire lifetime god cannot figure out if a man is good or not. Interviewers try doing this in under an hour in the course of a couple of conversations. After the debacle with the manufacturing candidate, while recruiting for senior positions, I use a different approach. I ask the person to whiteboard his strategy and plans for the role envisaged, and discuss it with him threadbare. Some unanswered questions always remain. I then request the candidate to flesh out a few pages on how he would go about setting up something from scratch. The process of thinking at this level and detailing a plan sometimes makes it obvious to the candidate that although he may be an expert in his area of work, building a business is a very different game. It asks for financial understanding, deal-making capability, competitive knowledge, and the ability to identify a crack in a wall and make an opportunistic entry. For me, as the recruiter, it is a highly illuminating exercise. In the pages the candidate produces I get to see how his mind works. At the same time he begins to understand how I think, how I may be able to add value, and both of us get to experience the process of co-creation of what may become a business plan. But a business plan is not what gives a business its identity, its soul. So I invariably ask the individual to tell me about the one thing he thinks he has left to do in his life. The answer to this is always most telling. People who do not have an uplifting personal vision to achieve something will not be able to create memorability, which is what building a business is all about.

Whenever I think of this concept, I remember Ram Mohan, the man who helped Mindtree set up its infrastructure management services business. Ram Mohan had prior experience in building capability in that area, first for a large company where he worked for many years and then as a co-founder of a venture capital-funded entity that closed down. During our meeting, I asked Ram what he felt he had yet to achieve in his life. He replied that on his first attempt the infrastructure management business he created for the large company he had worked for grew to become a $20 million business by the time he moved out. Then he did it all over again, this time as an entrepreneur. Somehow, the second business closed down when its earnings had just about touched the $20 million level. Ram said that his life's dream was to break that jinx. He wanted to build a business that would touch $100 million in size. I instantly liked the idea; he did not need to say anything more. I was hardly surprised when Ram went on to build us a business that grew to be $100 million in size, and continues to grow.

However good the initial meetings, the white-boarding and the concept notes, and irrespective of how much you like the person, reference checks on a candidate's professional background are a must. The more senior the person, the greater the need for the specific department head or a leader of the organization to do the checks instead of the HR department doing it. Only people closely involved with the candidate's area of work can ask a referee probing questions and read the silences between sentences. When I conduct such meetings, I ask for guidance from the referee on how the candidate likes to be managed. What conditions bring out the best in him? When do the red flags go up? I don't just ask for opinions; I ask for narratives. I request the referee to tell me about instances and interactions. The depth and seriousness of the reference check eventually reaches the candidate via the referee and in itself communicates the professional environment in the company and the attention to detail that will be expected of the candidate if he is recruited into the organization.

While bringing a senior person on board, it is important to ensure that the individual knows as much about the hiring organization as the organization knows about him. It is a good idea to ask the person to do a reference check of his own. Such a thing goes well beyond the information pack that might have been provided or details that the organization's website may have. Additionally, an arranged weekend visit to the workplace, a phone conversation between the candidate and a customer, or a breakfast meeting with an independent board member or an investor go a long way in setting the stage for a good relationship.

There are times when, in spite of everything looking good during the days of courtship, a feeling that something is not quite right continues to disturb the recruiter. The cardinal principle in such an instance is: When in doubt, don't hire.

At a particular stage in Mindtree's life, we seriously considered starting a Knowledge Process Outsourcing (KPO) business. While looking for the right person to head the new business, we went through several rounds of interviews with an eminently qualified and experienced candidate in his late thirties from a large, well-respected company. When the time came for reference checks I was underwhelmed by the quality of referees he produced. Something was not falling into place. I couldn't ignore a strange feeling that he seemed too good to be true. Then we had a final meeting with him. Here, I asked him one last question: How would he measure success when he was 50?

'I want to be the richest man around,' he said.

I sat up. There was nothing wrong with that ambition, but Mindtree wasn't the company that would make it happen. I told him as much. He then retracted his statement and clarified that he hadn't meant what he said. This was a double whammy because it showed that he had not taken me seriously when he answered my question. In the end, we didn't hire him because he had cast a shadow of doubt in my mind about his commitment and approach to working at Mindtree. Years later, it gave me no pleasure to hear that the person had made a number of wrong career moves and had moved away from the mainstream corporate world.

At times a recruiter may end up interviewing candidates who are eminently qualified and experienced in their own areas of discipline, the minute details of which the recruiter may not understand. There may be technicalities galore in the work the candidate does, but it is best not to get swayed by this. The recruiter needs to be alert to the nuances of his answers and ask himself the questions: Is there a telltale sign I am glossing over? Am I being too eager to hire? If the gut feeling about the candidate is a 'no', then go with it. The candidate may be a Nobel Laureate, but the money going to him is your organization's.

Once on board, the mistake all hiring companies make is to quickly forget the new joinee. In a week's time he might begin to look familiar to everyone in the organization but the new workplace will still seem unfamiliar to him. When you uproot and replant professionals, particularly those in senior positions, they wilt before they take root. Three things can be done at this time to help them fit in quickly and function better. Personally introduce them to their peers to establish credentials on both sides and create lifelines. Set up a 90-day plan and have him sign off on it to remove surprises and false expectations. Finally, meet him formally once every 30 days to check if things are working out. This will ensure that the organization remains invested in the success of the newcomer.

■

As an organization scales, there will arise the inevitable situation that requires people in positions of seniority and consequence to be fired. Many find the task uncomfortable, but when such situations arise the organization's needs get priority over individual concerns.

At the time when the Y2K hype was waning, Indian IT Services companies were in a frenzy, looking for new opportunities, and every one of them was seized by the need to open offices overseas, mostly in the US. Simultaneously, the need arose to hire locals to sell in that market. It was felt that an American (read Caucasian) selling to an American would find greater success in this – the accent, the baseball stories and the barbecue small talk would be just right. Then the conversation went one step further: the mega deals would require the recruitment of a local head, preferably from a company like IBM or one of the Big Four (PricewaterhouseCoopers, Deloitte, Ernst & Young and KPMG).

During that period of part naiveté, part good intent, an Indian mid-size company took on someone fitting that profile to head their US office. No one flinched at his huge compensation because a higher number made them feel good about netting just the right fish that would bring in the fortune. However, before the man brought in business, he brought in his secretary and a few other cohorts from his past life, and expensive entertainment bills (big business is done at the golf course, right?). The company's gross margin soon headed south, but everyone exulted that the big catch would come along soon; after all, this man's promises weren't about the minnows! The first quarter went by and then the next. Then a year had passed without anything much to talk about. It was then that the bosses back in India slowly, reluctantly at first, broached the topic among themselves.

To cut a long story short, they realized they had made a mistake. But now the bigger issue was how to fire the guy. Who would do it? What about the protracted, multi-million-dollar lawsuit that could potentially follow? After much agonized discussion, the No. 2 man in the company was dispatched to the US. He spent good money to get a lawyer's opinion and understand the steps involved in firing an American national. Frantic calls were exchanged between him and the situation room back in India. Finally, the day of reckoning arrived. After some rehearsal and with deep trepidation, our man cleared his throat, knocked on his American colleague's door, entered hesitatingly, wished him, took a seat, gathered all his courage and delivered the news: 'We regret it very much but we no longer require your services.' The man received the message calmly and replied, 'I wonder what took you so long!' Then he turned around to empty the drawers and left uneventfully.

Yes, letting people go might involve occasional complications. In some cases, there may be national regulations in place, and if the individual's contract with an organization has a severance clause the organization had better know what it is dealing with. But no management should be afraid to fire non-performance; it is the most absurd fear to have. Performance and failure to perform are professional issues. They have nothing to do with the colour of a person's skin or his nationality. If the reason is not related to performance but has something to do with breach of integrity, sexual harassment or a similar issue that brings disrepute to the profession and the organization, the offender should be fired without fear of consequence, including loss of business.

There are three themes that recur when someone at a senior level is fired. Sometimes these co-exist. One, and almost uniformly, the person giving the marching orders is greeted with hurt. Two, the individual being fired is taken aback because while the management believed that he hadn't delivered, he felt otherwise, and may have even thought that he had been called in to discuss a career progression. Three, and this one is when an upstart is faced with the news that he is being fired, the management may get a mouthful and be threatened that the lawyers are going to come soon. In 99 per cent of such cases, there are no lawyers. It is just a lot of bark, and the greater the bark the less intense the bite. The guy who will really send the lawyers will not reveal this information upfront.

In conclusion, fire with reason, fire as the thought-through last resort, fire if you must, fire with fairness, take expert help, be reasonable, keep in mind the indignity the person being fired may suffer in such a situation and be cognizant of the material difficulty the person may have to face. Customize the severance (not one size fits all) particularly if the individual has served you well at some stage but has now become deadwood. Irrespective of the part of the world you are in, keep a document trail. And, most importantly, fire without trembling. In business, it isn't a good idea to be afraid.

16

ARE YOU BUOYANT?

> 'Managing people is not the responsibility of the HR department alone. As necessary as the HR department may be, it cannot replace the leader's responsibility and capacity to build engagement and nurture talent.'

IT IS PARTICULARLY DURING an inflection point, when the organization wants to break through the clouds, that people will tell you scale comes at a great cost: Employees become a commodity in the organization. Leaders become impersonal. The intimacy between the leaders and employees fades away and the disconnect cascades down the organizational structure.

It need not be that way. Leadership proximity, an essential requirement for creating 'buoyancy', a state that the organization experienced in its initial years when everyone gave their best and every new endeavour was an adventure, can exist comfortably right through a company's growth. Of course, it requires continuous work, but which good thing in life does not?

The good news for leaders is that maintaining close relations with employees is not rocket science. A few things done well by a leader is sufficient to keep an enterprise feeling organically whole. But it must start with a basic tenet that the leader should internalize: managing people is not the responsibility of the HR department alone. As necessary as the HR department may be, it cannot replace the leader's responsibility and capacity to build engagement and nurture talent. There are simple ways in which leaders can ascertain commitment, loyalty, efficiency and productivity among their employees, and eventually sustained excellence and growth for the organization.

It begins with the leader spending one-on-one, quality time with key employees. This is different from a problem-solving session, or having fun in a company picnic or an off-site group exercise. 'White space time', as it is called, is characterized by the absence of an agenda. Choosing a time and environment when there are no distractions and the conversation can be relaxed and effortless opens the doors to many interesting outcomes. This can happen while travelling to another city to attend a meeting, or while visiting a tradeshow, or attending a training programme together. The sheer act of learning together can build shared foresight and bring forth a subliminal idea or question that can go on to benefit the organization in the long run. White space time invariably builds intimacy and trust between leader and employee, both necessary for the organization to flourish.

Often, employees have no idea about the thoughts and points of action engaging the leader between the statement of objectives in the beginning of the year and an analysis of the quarter-end results. Transparency is key. It is important for a leader to regularly publish what is on his mind to the entire set of next-level employees. During my days as the Chief Operating Officer (COO) at Mindtree, I used to have a whiteboard in my office. I used it to write my to-do list. It started as a visual management system to record reminders and take weekly stock of the tasks that had got done and ones that were still in the works. Among other things, it made for an entertaining game like knots-and-crosses or Jumble, which are also satisfying and energy-giving when you complete them. I also used the whiteboard for brainstorming, jotting down the points I wanted to address in an employee communication or a client proposal, and to make the board come alive I used different-coloured markers for the different categories of thought I put down. Gradually, I realized that the whiteboard was having a profound impact on the people who reported to me. Whenever they entered my room, their eyes would first go over what was on the board, noting what might have changed. It became clear to me that the board told them at a glance what I was preoccupied with. Invariably it involved them because they were the people I turned to to get things done. As a result, a lock-step was created and they developed anticipative skills. They started predicting how my to-do list might impact them, then they figured out the interdependencies with their colleagues, and set out to complete tasks with no supervision on my part. As time went by, I noticed that the people who reported to me were in turn publishing what was on their minds to those whom they supervised. The cascading process soon started to build buoyancy in the organization.

Leaders are often not aware that most people pretty much run on their own steam and appreciate an 'on-demand' supervisor who is available when they need him rather than someone who will take over their job and do it for them. The leader's primary objective is then to make sure that the employees have the resources they require to perform their tasks most efficiently, and that while they may be stretching themselves to get things done, they are certainly not killing themselves in the process. In short, his goal should be to train people how to fish, not to feed them.

As the organization scales, and volume and complexity overtakes everyone's lives, a leader can contribute to productivity and efficiency in the organization in three distinct ways.

The first is by critically questioning teams that are about to begin a project. Here the leader plays a very important role because, while the head of marketing or finance or HR is an expert in the particular area of operation, only the leader, one-time removed from the task at hand, can ask a set of 'what-if' questions that will enable everyone to see the big picture. The leader might know less about the particulars of a job than the people on the team but he has a wider perspective on the business as a whole. It is precisely this outside-in view, this arm's length, that gives him the chance to ask probing questions that can help the team to assess if they are missing something that could make them more successful in their efforts, to ascertain that their plan is the most efficient among alternatives, and perhaps even to arrive at crucial solutions where they may have reached a dead end earlier.

The second is by means of performance reviews that are planned ahead and conducted formally across the organization. Being structured, it helps the leader and the employee to reaffirm their shared understanding of key goals, acknowledge the present status of their work, discuss calibration and ask for help. Some leaders take the review mechanism for granted and postpone it indefinitely. You travelled together last week, so it need not be done. Wrong. You had so much to do in this quarter, you could always push it to the next quarter. Wrong. Why not combine it with the appraisal discussion?

Dead wrong. It is essential that the review be conducted as planned. Some leaders who are regular and disciplined about the review still need help to make the review effective. Both leader and employee need to look upon the review meeting as a mini board meeting, where the leader is the board and the employee the CEO of his sphere. This is an evaluative meeting, rather than a 'we are in this together' discussion. Many senior executives I know believe that the tougher the review the better they perform in their tasks ahead.

While the first two interactions occur at specific times, periodic feedback from the leader is critical in building a productive relationship. Everyone knows this but few act on it. Sometimes leaders refrain from delivering hard feedback because they are afraid of the fallout. If they feel they really need to address issues, they wait until the annual appraisal discussion to do it. I grew up in a lower-middle-class home where we had a few rules. These were always about small things: returning from home before sunset; not hanging out with kids who didn't take their work seriously; not borrowing even the smallest amount of money from others. If these rules were violated, the feedback was instantaneous, and whoever gave it did so without worrying about consequences. The same principle applies to the workplace. Regular feedback reinforces values and purpose, brings clarity on expectations and enables people to work better. Postponed feedback always gets diluted, becomes burdensome and has little learning value.

If a leader is a critical questioner and reviewer, he must also be the ultimate sense-maker. In the second phase of growth when the stakes are higher and the risks greater, it is important to remember that this is a new journey both for the senior employees who have signed up for the next phase and for the most recent lateral hire. There are chances that they may be equally confused about issues from time to time and have constant doubts. When people are confused, they are often likely to make use of what they think is useful knowledge, usually solutions from past experiences, that may be inadequate and sometimes even counterproductive in the current circumstances. When the doubts come forth, a leader must know that the competent employee is not seeking an answer. He is seeking a sense-maker who can help him figure out the key to solving the puzzle: Why are we where we are? Is what we are experiencing a mole hill or a mountain? Are there organizations out there who have gone through what we are going through? What can we learn from their experiences?

In showing them the way through a labyrinth of doubts, the leader's primary objective should be to reiterate the organization's vision and keep the organization healthy, productive, and always buoyant and ready to scale.

17

THE FASHION-DESIGNER NUN

> 'In today's world, it is no longer enough to learn from your customer, supplier and your competitor. The most impactful piece of knowledge could come from someone in a very different kind of business and, sometimes, someone not in business at all.'

THE SUN TEMPLE AT Konark on the eastern coast of India, famously known as the Black Pagoda, is a thirteenth-century wonder. A World Heritage Site, it is one of the most awe-inspiring works created by man in the history of civilization. Today, the main temple stands destroyed; only the front remains. Despite that, the sheer size and beauty of the existing structure evokes wonder.

Story has it that King Narasimha Deva I had ordered his prime minister, Sibei Santara (whose real name was probably Siba Samantaray), to oversee the design and construction of a magnificent temple as a tribute to the Sun God. The temple was to be designed such that the first ray of the rising sun illuminated the sanctum sanctorum and, for this to happen, the location for its construction was carefully chosen. However, there was a hitch. The temple had to be built on the shoreline and land would have to be reclaimed from the sea by dropping cartloads of massive boulders at the spot. Unfortunately, every time the king's men attempted this strong waves devoured the boulders. Clueless about a solution to the problem, Sibei Santara travelled around for days, lost in thought. At some point during his meanderings, he got hungry and came across the hut of a poor old lady. He asked for food, and the old lady served him some hot porridge. In his haste to begin eating, the prime minister dipped his fingers right in the middle of the plate to scoop out some porridge. Instantly, he jerked away his hand in shock and pain. The old lady chided him for his foolishness. 'You are as stupid as that man Sibei Santara,' she said. The prime minister was taken aback, but curious. 'Why do you call him stupid? Tell me about him, Mother,' he said. The old lady told him how, under Sibei Santara's directions, the king's men were foolishly dumping boulders into the sea just as he had put his fingers into the middle of the bowl of hot porridge. They should be working the periphery, not the centre, she told him. Just like the way to eat hot porridge was by starting at the periphery, the way to claim land was to begin at the shore and extend into the sea.

■

> 'Whatever got you where you are today, won't take you where you want to go tomorrow.'
>
> 'You must learn newer ways of doing things, and new things to do.'
>
> 'To solve complex problems, you must think outside the box.'

These are some of the most quoted sentences on solving problems and getting new ideas to get ahead in the organizational context. Management teachers and consultants do not tire of urging professionals to embrace these mantras if they want to break through the clouds. Frankly, these pearls of wisdom usually remain what they are – pleasant to the ear – and hardly ever get implemented. Very few people, for example, know how to think 'out of the box'. Where would you start if you were told to? What would you do?

The starting point to thinking out of the box is to step outside it. If Sibei Santara had not stepped out, he wouldn't have arrived at the solution to his problem. That said, unlike the prime minister of old, in the organizational context we are continuously besieged by issues, and out-of-the-box ideas don't just come when we need them. Stepping out of the box, thinking differently and coming up with unique solutions cannot be on-demand activities. They need to be made an integral part of an organization's culture. Employees should love the concept and practice it all the time. Not just when a big customer is threatening to desert the organization and switch over to the biggest competitor.

When an organization embraces this kind of thinking it can benefit in two distinct ways. One is to look around and see what its customers, suppliers and competitors are doing and mimic their best practices. The other is building perspective. The latter is not about spotting a specific idea here or a best practice there. It is about appreciating how others think. This is the more powerful approach. It creates the mental space for ideas to grow on ideas.

When Ramesh Gopalakrishnan, one of Mindtree's senior-most technical leaders, was trying to figure out how to teach Mindtree's project groups the Agile methodology of tackling software projects, he went to the Sparsh Hospital in Bengaluru which has an Advanced Trauma Centre. For those who do not know, traditionally, the software development lifecycle follows what is called the Waterfall model in which things happen in a somewhat linear manner. Simply put, first you get the user's requirements and create the design. After that you draw up the architecture and then develop the software. Once the software is developed, a team tests it for form and functionality, its ability to deliver a secure computing environment, its ability to scale when usage is high, and other such facets. At the end of the testing phase, the software is deployed. Unless one step is complete, the subsequent steps do not get activated. This means that the various teams, starting with the one that collects information about the user's requirements all the way to the one that oversees deployment of the finished software, work with a lot of time in hand to be able to do things step by step. Central to the development and deployment of industrial-grade software is how team members share knowledge, exchange ideas, question each other, and how formal reviews take place. Large-scale applications often take years to develop using the Waterfall model and get completed in a structured manner involving immense amounts of formalism and documentation.

All that is changing now, thanks to the rapid growth of internet-based applications. Think of Google. It is changing its form and functionality almost every day. People at Google are watching users use applications on the Google platform and rapidly reconfiguring the site based on usage patterns. Behind it all is an environment of a concurrent build–test–deploy process. No longer are projects being completed sequentially. Sometimes applications are developed even before the complete user requirements are known. Similarly, the testing teams work in an anticipative manner to develop a test plan well before any coding is done. In such situations, the traditional Waterfall model slows things down and this is why the Agile methodology is used.

The Agile methodology, as its name suggests, does away with the sequential approach. Every step in the lifecycle of a project using this methodology is simultaneous. Software professionals need to work very differently here from how they would in a traditional Waterfall team. There is a high degree of parallelism and teams collapse the know–do gap. This method does not involve prolonged project reviews in conference rooms backed by meticulously developed slides and bulky documentation. Everyone in the team has access to knowledge at the same time and at high speed because user-needs change constantly and the window of opportunity to read the customers' need and satisfy it is very small.

Now think of the medical team in a trauma hospital. The doctors and the supporting staff cannot predict when, how and in what shape the patient will arrive. Sometimes not one but a number of accident or trauma victims may get wheeled in at the same time. As soon as an emergency call is received, before the ambulance has arrived, the diagnosis begins on the basis of reports from the ambulance staff. Upon arrival of the patients, different teams get to work concurrently, and often need to change their plans on the fly depending on changing requirements. Throughout this critical period, team members constantly exchange information so that every person on duty is aware of what the other is doing and is updated on each new development. There is a high degree of simultaneity in the way the teams function, and constant knowledge gathering and instant decision-making takes place based on information that arrives in real time. Trauma teams collaborate in a cross-disciplinary manner; their ability to work in harmony can make the difference between life and death for the patient. In other words, they must work in the most 'agile' manner anyone can imagine. For this, every morning, the doctors lock themselves in for what is called a scrum meeting.

A scrum meeting is mandatory as the doctors on duty at the Advance Trauma Centre start their day. They congregate in a small meeting room to discuss the cases from the previous day. Every doctor presents his or her case(s) and talks about what went right and what went wrong, the interventions that were made and the reasons for making them. The details are projected as radiographic images on the wall and peers give instant feedback, including criticism and questioning, which can sometimes be quite severe.

The scrum sessions are the most vital and rapid way to distribute knowledge in a system that cannot deal with long waits. Once Ramesh and his team had studied how Sparsh Hospital runs these sessions, they explained to our project teams how scrum meetings were impacting the way the hospital dealt with medical emergencies. If scrum sessions were making a difference in a world where lives depended upon the outcome of the meeting, their efficacy in the world of software, far less volatile than a hospital's emergency and trauma ward, would get immediate results. This was not a case of picking up a specific practice from another discipline and applying it; it was about picking up perspective.

As organizations scale, the need to learn from unusual sources becomes paramount because everyone else in the business has already tapped into the usual sources. In today's world it is no longer enough to learn from your customer, supplier and your competitor; sometimes the most impactful piece of knowledge could come from someone in a very different kind of business or perhaps from someone not in business at all.

I have always believed that the Missionaries of Charity is one of the earliest, most successful and rare 'multinationals' in India. It is present in 133 countries around the world where the sisters of the charity run homes for newborn babies, patients suffering from HIV/AIDS, tuberculosis, leprosy, and the destitute.

Why should this be significant? Consider this: each wing of the organization functions in sync with the other. It is able to manage a huge workforce with the associated complexities of recruitment, and specific training and development. It is evidently in control of its supply chain management, funding, book-keeping, liaising with dozens of external agencies and a million other things that must be done concurrently, from changing the linen in a leprosy patient's bed to feeding a newborn baby. For all that, it does not use an ERP package, or even the internet for information management.

I once asked a diminutive, frail sister why the organization did not use computers and she promptly chastised me. 'We cannot have a computer here, we work with the poor,' she said. When I pointed to the archaic black telephone on the table, she dismissed me with, 'Oh, the poor are not scared of the telephone. They are used to it.' No arguments with that. Now imagine running a 24/7 organization across 133 countries, with a permanent workforce of more than 5,000 sisters with just a telephone.

Quite obviously, there is a very advanced planning system at work here. The nuns are transferred from one location to another every three years. The location of the next posting is not known to a nun until twenty-four hours before she has to move. She is also unaware before this time about the tasks she will be handling at her new posting. A nun who is specialized in geriatric care may get rotated to a home for children or a care centre for HIV/AIDS patients. Each rotation requires very different skills, from attending to human needs to the more technical areas of maintaining inventory and infrastructure. The Missionaries of Charity has a well-managed multi-skilling programme in place that plans ahead to provide specialized training for the sisters. Again, a nun who functions as the Sister Superior at one location may serve under another superior on her next assignment, who may well be junior to her in age and in her years of being with the Missionaries of Charity. Thus, an apparently simple matter of moving a nun from one location to another is in reality a complex human resources exercise because of the interdependence of the nuns' skills, locations and roles.

Once, I visited a children's home run by the Missionaries of Charity in Kochi. This home receives newborn babies, some of whom are abandoned by unwed mothers. As I explored the first floor of the home, I was particularly impressed by a highly energetic nun who was simultaneously looking after half a dozen babies. Afterwards, while I was sitting in the courtyard downstairs chatting with a few other sisters, the nun I had seen earlier came running by, wiping her hands on her apron. She had just finished bathing and feeding the babies and was now going to attend a course in fashion design, she said.

'You mean tailoring?' I asked her. 'Fashion design' somehow did not sound appropriate for the home.

'No, no. It is *fashion design*. These days, no one wants tailoring anymore,' she replied as she rushed off.

Another nun explained the full story to me. Quite often an unwed mother shows up with a newborn at their doorstep. While the baby is received and cared for, the sisters do not let the mother go back to uncertainty. Most of the unwed mothers are poor and are not educated, making them easy prey for exploitation. The sisters, therefore, shelter these women for some time and rehabilitate them by teaching them vocational skills so that they do not become vulnerable again. The nun I had just met was on her way to attend a train-the-trainer programme in fashion design!

From Sibei Santara to the trauma care unit of the Sparsh Hospital to the Missionaries of Charity, there are lessons to learn from everywhere. To identify them and imbibe them appropriately we need to take the act of thinking 'out of the box' out of a conference room into the real world. It must become an exercise that is routine in our organizations. That is when the organization's collective 'mind' will attain the capacity to expand and unusual new ideas will emerge – ideas that go beyond best practices to create what management thinker C.K. Prahalad called 'next practices'.

18

SQUARE PEGS AND ROUND HOLES

> Just as you rely on a specialist to diagnose your medical problems, so too with the talent pool in your organization. A growth-seeking organization can achieve acceleration only with the right kind of driver behind the wheel.

THE ATTRIBUTES THAT MAKE a great athlete are very different from those a renowned author may possess. We understand this well in our personal lives, but seem to lose our grasp on the metaphor when it comes to people in our organizations.

When an organization has reached the point at which it is raring to take on the world as a young adult, its people need to ask themselves a set of fundamental questions: Five years out, what kind of company do we want to be seen as? What are the leadership attributes that are needed to build such a company? How do we know if these attributes exist in our current set of leaders and the ones that will follow?

The last question flows from those that precede it and the answer is not easy to find without expert help. Organizations may recognize the advantages of bringing in external expertise in conducting market research, design and testing, and internal and external satisfaction surveys, but they don't seem to be aware of the immense value experts bring to the assessment of leadership attributes.

At Mindtree we invested a great deal in leadership development. A big reason for the company reaching its IPO stage was the quality of its second-level leaders, who had been carefully groomed. But by the time we hit $300 million in revenue, up from $100 million at the time we went public, we started feeling that we did not know what leadership attributes the organization needed *today* to become the company we envisioned five years from now. That is when we once again defined a Mindtree for the future, at a broad, conceptual and qualitative level by polling our people. Then, with the help of an external agency, in this case Korn/Ferry, we settled on four clusters of attributes that needed to be nurtured in the present for Mindtree to successfully reach its future destination.

The clusters were named Ninja, Coach, Thought-Leader and Rainmaker.

A Ninja is a first-rate implementer. Give him a task and rest assured that the work will get done, on-time, on-budget. You do not have to second guess or supervise the person.

In delivering on the commitment, he will not bend rules. In short, he is every boss's dream subordinate. Now think of the Coach. He is always available. He never competes with his team. He is the go-to person everyone feels comfortable with, the sense-maker, the one helping people solve their problems, rejoicing in their growth, forever giving of his own knowledge and experience. Now the third category: the Thought-Leader. This is the individual who questions the status quo. He has a definite point of view, is able to articulate it and gets everyone's attention. He is the think-tank of the organization and the soothsayer for its prospects. Finally, there is the Rainmaker, a first-rate creator of new opportunities. He is the one bringing in the big deal, the new client, making forays into hitherto uncharted areas of expertise. He can create something out of nothing.

Now that you know the four categories, I want you to do a simple, intuitive analysis of me, Subroto Bagchi. Never mind that you don't have all the data you need. From reading my book you must have formed an impression of me. If you were to choose two out of the four clusters of attributes which would you list as my primary and secondary characteristics? In order that you come to a conclusion on your own, I will change the subject and return to it later.

If I were to mark out a few significant initiatives during the last few years that helped Mindtree's people and the organization to scale, they would be the rebranding we did with Siegel+Gale, the leadership assessment exercise we did with Korn/Ferry, the business development capability assessment we did using an organization named Chally and, finally, an involved exercise that is afoot with Bain & Company to help us structure a Mindtree of the future. Here I will largely focus on the second and third as they are about assessing key talent.

In 2010, starting with KK and me, the top twenty people in the company were put through assessments to determine their strengths. Every leader had a primary and a secondary competence. When the evaluation was complete, we could see what kind of organization we were as well as identify the holes that could prevent us from scaling in the future. The results were astonishing at two levels. First, many leaders realized they had had no idea what their primary and secondary competence actually were. The second flowed from the first: roles that required certain kinds of leadership were being performed by people who did not have the attributes required. Neither they nor the organization was aware of the gap, and both ended up struggling with poor performance and sometimes even non-performance. This had nothing to do with the fact that the company was doing well. That came from the capacity we had built in the past. We were suddenly aware that the future we had in mind could require vastly different capabilities. The talent we had today could not guarantee future success. In effect, today we may need first-rate rabbits that run well but tomorrow we might well need eagles that fly.

Now, let us return to my question. What do you think are my primary and secondary competence? I often ask groups of leaders to guess this and in three years since the assessment first got done, only *one* person, literally among hundreds, has got it right. Well, my primary competence is being a Ninja; my secondary is being a Rainmaker. Did I know that in my decades of working? No, I didn't. I, like most of you probably have, saw myself as a Thought-Leader and, in recent years, even as a Coach. But a Ninja? Heck, no.

After the assessment sank in and I sat back to think about it I realized how correct it was. My best performance has always been for someone else. From the time I was a three-year-old I was a great follower and not a blind one. I have always made my bosses look good; I have helped them succeed. Sometimes I have actually helped them build great vision that wasn't theirs in the beginning. In the end people knew it as theirs and when they became brilliant successes I was very happy being part of it. I also questioned my bosses. I disagreed with them without being disagreeable. I was no slacker. If I took on something, it got done. No ifs and buts there. Along the way, my bosses could sleep well knowing one thing: accepted processes would be respected right through. So, it all added up. I was a Ninja. While I gradually embraced the reality, most of the others struggled with the results of their assessments. Imagine a country head who isn't a Rainmaker, or a practice head who isn't a Thought-Leader, or a delivery head who is a poor Coach and as a result is unable to delegate, and burns out at both ends while his team feels alienated. Or think of an HR head who is inherently a Rainmaker but was given the job of a Ninja and asked to overhaul HR processes, a task that would need three years of committed work.

Related to the four clusters of leadership attributes were two sets of foundational abilities. One set was the different kinds of agility required of a leader. These were things like mental agility, people agility, change agility, and so on. The second set had to do with various categories of competence like task focus, energy, humility, self-confidence. We were assessed for these too.

When we looked at the data that flowed in, there were many revelations. One was about the collective personality of Mindtree, that is, the most dominant characteristics of our people. The data showed that we were largely a Ninja company. On the positive side, that made us first-rate when it came to execution; we are such a task-focused organization that when the company was boiling over the smartphone fiasco that almost shut us down, the field and delivery divisions of the organization (mercifully) had no clue about the upheaval. In the most gruesome, near-death year of our existence, our topline grew, we added new accounts and not one customer was negatively impacted. But this Ninja set-up would not be able to transform our dream of Mindtree in 2020 into reality. Our vision required Rainmakers and Thought-Leaders to be in positions of leadership more than ever before.

But what about the existing leaders? We learnt some very basic things about dealing with presently capable, loyal leaders who were not natural fits for the positions they held. If we identified a country head who was a Thought-Leader and Coach we did not have to show him the door. We needed to make sure that the individual played to his strengths, and then surround him with an able and supportive team of Rainmakers. Without the benefit of the assessment, we would not have known that dissimilar people are a better mutual fit and that similarity can lead to comfortable mediocrity.

The Korn/Ferry assessment opened our eyes to another interesting aspect of organizational behaviour. Mindtree, it seemed, was a 'complex creative' organization. We loved a complex problem and we loved engaging with it until we had brilliantly solved it and then we looked for the next great complex problem. But, know what? Our competition was laughing all the way to the bank doing less complex work. So preoccupied were we with the kind of business we wanted that we missed the fact that simple is smart; that the world's purpose is not to have complex problems so that we could solve them.

What happens when leaders of a complex creative company get together? They debate every issue; they lose track of time. They forget that the brilliant execution of a simple idea is more valuable and more profitable than a complex problem solved with agonizing perfection. The former helps the organization to scale; the latter slows it down.

Close on the heels of the leadership assessment, we went on to do a similar assessment of our business development division. This time we chose to work with another specialist organization, Chally. To my surprise, there was some discomfort regarding this in the minds of our salespeople. Were we stereotyping them through assessments? What would we do with those who did not fit into the mental model we established for their roles? In order to make them comfortable, KK and I decided that we would get assessed first and share our findings with them.

The Chally assessment focused on figuring out whether a salesperson was a hunter or a farmer, concepts I've written about earlier in the book. Like the Korn/Ferry assessment, the Chally assessment showed that we had many instances of hunters who were lazily farming, while farmers were hunting with a plough and getting eaten up by the competition.

After the two initial assessments, we got progressively better at identifying people for specific positions. Earlier we used to select people for performance and leadership roles based on years and years of internal assessments, 360-degree feedback and, sometimes, their track records. Now we referred to the assessment data. The data is not solely conclusive; it is a diagnostic view that you don't want to miss. But more than using the diagnostic report to find a 'cure', we applied it extensively to engineer wellness. Based on the results, we went to great lengths to create customized development plans for every leader with a runway, got some of them personal coaches, put them through long-acting group exercises. Along the way, we also let go of a few people. It wasn't easy, but we did it without bias or disaffection of any kind.

Assessments are powerful tools. There are excellent organizations out there with the wisdom gleaned from working with hundreds and thousands of professionals across industries and geographies that can bring to bear the knowledge required for effective talent management in any company wanting to get to the next level. Just as you rely on a specialist to diagnose your medical problems, or decide your nutrition plan or gym routine, so too with the talent pool in your organization. Being guided by experts in this matter can hugely benefit a growth-seeking organization where acceleration is important and can be achieved with the right kind of driver behind the wheel.

Meanwhile, look in the mirror. You may be an eagle even though you love the idea of donning the rabbit's fur.

19

GARDENING TALES

> 'You may have good people among your second rung of leaders, and they may be inherently cerebral, but they won't scale into larger, organization-wide roles unless someone tells them to shed their skin.'

UNTIL MINDTREE ENTERED ITS post-IPO phase, we were largely a founder-led company. But at a critical juncture it was time for us to consider what was to come next. Who did we want to become in the coming decade? Where did we want to go from here? And, most importantly, who were the people who would take us there?

As we pondered over and discussed these questions, it became clear to us that our ambitions for the organization required expanding our leadership capacity beyond the founders, not just to execute our vision but to envision and co-create Mindtree's future. In my mind, I saw a decade of transition from founders to non-founders. This would mean handing over our knowledge and skills to a set of leaders waiting in the wings. That is how my assignment as the Gardener of Mindtree took root.

Why Gardener, you may ask. Working with people is somewhat like tending to a garden. It is a long-acting process; there is no instant gratification here. In a garden, the trees do not wake up every day and serve the gardener; it is always the other way around. The trees do not come to see the gardener where he may be; the gardener goes wherever the trees are. He knows each plant intimately, and customizes his attention. He knows their individual nutritional needs and pruning requirements, and how to fight the bugs and beetles. He can tell a weed from a useful plant and a useful insect from a pest.

I started off by doing three things: I quit my role as the COO to be able to give full-time attention to the task. I identified a set of leaders from the 100 senior-most employees beyond the founders who I thought would be ready to work with me and would potentially benefit. Then I got down to creating a methodology of sorts. The experience of working with some of these high-achieving women and men gave me invaluable insight into building leadership capacity for the future, an exercise that is essential for every growing organization.

Before I present some of these, a few words about an

important question: How do you measure the success of such an endeavour? When I thought about it, the answer dawned on me in the form of a rather simple equation. I was setting myself up for personalized, close engagement with 100 chosen Mindtree leaders over a period of time. I told myself that I would assume that 50 per cent of the leaders I work with may eventually leave Mindtree; 25 per cent would stay on but experience no significant benefit; another 15 per cent would receive only marginal benefits. That would leave 10 per cent to unlock their inner potential in a significant way. What we would then have is a set of ten outstanding leaders. Even if each one built a $200 million business over the next ten years, we would have a $2 billion enterprise. Not a bad Return on Investment (ROI) at all. It was a numbers game of a different kind!

Returning to the lessons, the first one I learnt while engaging with second-rung leaders was about big-picture thinking. In the initial phases of a start-up and through the first phase of growth, it is invariably the handful of people right at the top who think of the big picture. The key job of the stars at the next level is to execute with perfection. But in the years that pass, this works like a double-edged sword. As involved and knowledgeable as people might be about their respective silo, when the time comes to scale it becomes apparent that they have difficulty in envisioning the battlefield in its entirety. The

R&D guy will be blank on gross margins and profitability; the head of HR will not know about delivery or manufacturing; the finance head will be clueless about the top three customers and the challenges of working with them. Of more concern is the fact that all of them will probably draw a blank if asked: Where do you see the industry heading ten years from now? What are five major trends that will emerge in our industry in the coming years? What are your thoughts on the most significant discontinuities? What in your view are the factors that could cause our business to bite the dust? They may know a little about some of these issues but it is now time for them to develop the ability for critical questioning and forming a point-of-view of their own beyond what the Forresters and Gigas and Gartners have said. You may have good people among your second rung of leaders, and they may be inherently cerebral, but they won't scale into larger, organization-wide roles unless someone tells them to shed their skin.

The need for big-picture thinking directly leads us to the idea of visioning. In the beginning, there is usually one visionary and an entire organization lines up behind the tip of the arrow. In the next phase of growth, a single arrow will not work; the organization will need an arrow made of arrows. The capacity to create a vision will now have to become fractal. It starts with self-awareness. Many second-level leaders find it difficult to answer the basic questions, 'Who am I?' and 'Who will I be 5 years from now?' Viktor Frankl, the author of *Man's Search for Meaning*, explains in his book how important it is to have something as-yet-unfinished, something to look forward to achieving or completing, for human beings to make their lives meaningful. People who do not possess a personal vision or purpose will find it impossible to build an organizational vision. The ability required for the two is the same: you have to be able to see a future that does not exist.

A vision is not a plan. It does not come factory-fitted with a navigation device. Along the way, you may lose your bearings, the terrain may throw up surprises and a hundred other things may make the journey difficult. Leaders in the making have to master the ability to learn as they go along, and pass on their learning to others. Yet, unexpectedly, the learning ability of many potential leaders slows down dramatically mid-career despite stellar education and past professional success. One of the biggest stumbling blocks they face in rekindling their learning abilities is a personal insecurity about giving up their current level or position of success. A sales manager cannot learn product management if he cannot see beyond his no-cap sales incentives. A manufacturing star cannot learn about skill development unless he is open to occasionally changing his location. Allowing such insecurities to come in the way of physical and mental displacement, both of which are key for rapid, new learning, stalls growth in an individual.

Working with high-achievers also introduced me to an aspect that need not have come as a surprise but for the fact that these were people who were known to walk on water, so to speak. They did, except in some matters. In these matters, they were not just ordinary but were also afraid to be seen as ordinary and were therefore reluctant to seek help when they needed it. If you are a star in your organization but have ordinary needs, fears, anxieties and vulnerabilities, you are not alone. If you manage stars, you are certain to encounter this side to them.

Many young leaders are not comfortable with their inner self and believe that it has nothing to do with their professional side. This is a mistake. The way an individual negotiates a contract, recovers from a professional setback, defines risk-taking and acts on it, are all linked to what they are at their core. The idea of that self is often rooted in early childhood experiences. A person may have seen his parents part, another might have had an oppressive, excellence-seeking older member in the family, and someone else may have felt that a sibling was always unduly favoured. Then the person probably got busy with studies, excelled in academics, got the right jobs and courted success. Later, as these individuals begin to take on the pressures of leadership, they may find dealing with what they consider 'ordinary' emotions and insecurities frustrating and may perhaps even be afflicted by the fear of not being able to cope with them. It is best to tackle such situations in a straightforward manner. To a significant number of high-achievers I worked with, I had to say, 'Growing up means growing out of.' The beauty of the human brain is its plasticity. It can be trained and conditioned, and we can release ourselves from the clutches of our past if we want. Difficult though this may be, it is not impossible.

Many high-achievers also have an inaccurate understanding of their strengths and weaknesses. This may sound counterintuitive because we are speaking about successful people in positions of consequence. How can they not know their true strengths and weaknesses, you may ask. Well, they usually do. Except, in many cases, that knowledge is dated. The salesperson who was once a star is no longer that. The economy, market realities, nature of customers and indeed the product itself has changed. Unless he accepts the changed realities, he cannot either retrain himself or seek another area of strength that might give him a new lease of life. For a startling number of high-achievers, then, the professional graveyard may not be very far away.

A corollary to this is that many leaders have deep-seated, and often wrongly held notions, about their failings. These people overlook three possibilities. One, that what they were once not good at is possibly no longer a requirement for success. Imagine someone with bad handwriting fretting about it in the era of the keyboard! Second, that over the years they may have actually overcome the so-called inability or weakness, though they are unaware of it because they are stuck with an idea in their heads which no one else shares or knows about ('I do not make presentations as confidently as so-and so', or 'I don't do well in client-facing situations'). Third, that they might have become so respected among their peers because of many significant professional achievements that the so-called deficiency is not even noticed by anyone other than them ('I sometimes stammer when I cannot find the right word', or 'I am good at creating strategy but cannot execute it well'). The brilliant minds of high-acheivers sometimes prove to be a liability to them. When they get something wrong, they get it very wrong.

Many mid-career high-achievers suffer from a lack of self-awareness and are prone to be distracted by what they mistakenly view as a higher calling. They think about building a product of their own, becoming an entrepreneur, or even going away and starting a school someplace. These are certainly worthwhile things to do, but each one requires significant personal sacrifice, urgent commitment, focus and loyalty. There is no point in day-dreaming idly about an idea that is not rooted in reality and letting that become a distraction. It can make a person unfocused at a time when focus is very important.

There are many other facets in second-rung leaders that need to be kindled or killed before they can decisively move ahead and take charge of the future. To achieve this, what needs to be cultivated is an 'I am the new now' mindset that requires one major change: they must forget that they need a superior to be effective. This often proves difficult because they have always had someone to turn to, and now they have to be that someone. This brings along another interesting scenario. Most of these leaders have so far worked with people they have looked up to. But from this point onward the gap between them and those at the top is going to shrink. Suddenly they will be close enough to see the weaknesses and limitations in the people who have so far guided them. Many find this unnerving. It will take a little longer for them to understand that their superiors need not be smarter than them. That is why they are needed. The US President is one of the most powerful people in the world not because he is a perfect leader, but because he surrounds himself with outstanding men and women who make up for his shortcomings.

20

WHEN BRAHMA FAILS

> "The gods get it. Humans mostly do not. Often, the Brahmas of our world stay on after the act of creation, and instead of hiring Vishnu for the sustenance phase decide to do the job themselves, at times bringing the company's well-being into jeopardy."

THE HINDU PANTHEON IS ruled by the trinity of Brahma, Vishnu and Maheshwara. Bramha creates everything; Vishnu sustains and preserves; and Maheshwara is the destroyer of all order so that renewal can take place and the cycle of existence may continue. Our ancients who thought of this idea must have been management experts. Inherent in the idea are two things. One, the competence required to efficiently execute each of the three vital aspects – starting up, scaling and re-engineering – is qualitatively different. Two, the leadership mindset required for each is unique. Bramha would feel exasperated, even burnt out, doing Vishnu's job, and if Vishnu tried to discontinue a loss-making product line or fire the bottom 5 per cent on the performance scale he would surely mess things up. And don't ask me what would happen if a guy clothed in tiger skin with a live snake adorning his neck were to be given charge of the universe's sustenance.

The gods get it. Humans mostly do not. Often, the Brahmas of our world stay on after the act of creation, and instead of hiring Vishnu for the sustenance phase decide to do the job themselves. This has its dangers, the greatest of which is bringing the well-being of the organization into jeopardy.

Who gives birth to an enterprise? Of course, and without doubt, the answer is the entrepreneurial spirit, be it of an individual or a group. Without the strategic intent, passion, diligence and capacity to create scale that this individual or group possesses, high-growth organizations cannot be born. Unlike the Hindu trinity, in the case of some high-performance organizations founders who have stayed on have actually contributed to the organization's value and generated significant benefits for customers, employees and shareholders. Take the examples of Microsoft, Apple and Intel. Yet, there are countless instances of founders stalling an organization's growth and sometimes even driving their own creations into the ground by holding on to their positions and not bringing in professionals and fresh blood to lead (and not just run) their companies.

If you were being hired by a start-up, what would be your central worry? Without doubt you would be concerned about the competence of the founder, his vision for the organization and his work ethics. An awareness of such expectations creates a certain pressure on founders who might, as a result, begin an endless journey in search of personal excellence. While such a journey may be relevant to the initial phase of a company's operations, it becomes somewhat counter-productive once the organization has risen to the next level. At their core most founders remain doers who have withdrawal symptoms when they are not at work, and they forget that they are no longer required to be the most intelligent and capable problem-solvers in the organization. They continue to jump in to solve every problem, take charge of every other thing that needs attention. Some founders initially let go but soon reverse their position either because they feel 'jobless' or are overtaken by the urge to seize the joystick again because the plane is experiencing some turbulence and the new co-pilot is, well, new. When such behaviour perpetuates, it has a significant fallout. The managers below the founder in the organization's hierarchy may conveniently settle down in a neat arrangement in which all decisions and sometimes even actions are escalated. Who ends up making the brilliant presentation to the prospective client? Who is the one conducting the touch negotiation with a supplier? Who is trying to hold back an employee who has put in his papers? And who is concerned about the overuse of paper towels in the toilet? There is just one answer to all these questions. Sometimes, even if perfectly competent, proactive managers are employed in key positions, nothing in the company can happen without the matter being addressed to the founder. This automatically results in a slowing down of the decision-making process right through the organization, not to mention stifling the valuable experiences and opportunities that others could learn from.

In fact, founders have been known to hire less competent people than themselves, although more often than not this happens without their knowing it. They justify the conundrum by blaming both lack of talent in the market and the organization's inability to attract the right people, but it is really an unconscious affirmation that they are the ones who know best how to run the organization they have created.

Early success draws some founders into another very interesting trap – distraction. Consider Lakshmi. She is in her late thirties and runs a successful independent business. Believing that the time has come for her to improve her external network, she joins a group of high-performance, high-profile individuals from different organizations who are part of an elite club. In the first one or two get-togethers, the personalities of the other members, the quality of conversation, the spirited sharing of experiences make her feel that she has found an oasis. Then she is called upon to lead a sub-group and shines there. Soon, she is the vice-chairman of the group and has ended up committing a fortnight of her time planning the following year's trip to Istanbul where the members will listen to a retired secretary of state from the US, or the CEO of a big company who is known to one of the members, talking on strategy. Before she knows it, Istanbul has become her significant other, magical and inviting, and the squeaky-wheel customers and her organization's CFO, who is flagging poor collections in this quarter, are no longer a priority. Her hobby has now become her work and the primary recipient of her attention and energy is not the work for which she is paid.

Sometimes we miss the essence of myths by a mile. All of us know the story of Arjuna who focused only on the eye of the fish while taking his aim to pierce it and was successful at hitting his target and beating eminent opponents to win Draupadi's hand in marriage. Many do not know the story of the father of Zen Buddhism, Daruma, as he is known in Japan (though historically he can be identified as Bodhidharma, an Indian sage who lived during the fifth and sixth centuries BCE). Legend goes that Daruma went off to the forest to meditate for nine years. During this time he once accidentally fell asleep and was so furious with himself when he awoke that he cut off his eyelids to prevent himself from dropping off to sleep again. In Japan, the Daruma doll, a limbless, eyeless, brightly coloured doll, is considered the ultimate symbol of good luck and perseverence. At the beginning of a project the team involved brings in a Daruma doll and the team members together paint in one eye to mark the commencement of work. When the project is delivered, on or before time, fulfilling budgetary mandates, the entire team returns to paint the other eye to signal completion. In between, they remain focused and steadfast. The essence of the myth is simple: We cannot achieve our goals if we give in to distractions along the way.

In life, distraction does not always come as the newfound, compulsive love for golf or an invitation for a membership to an elite club. For some it may arrive in the form of over-ambition or over-confidence, which sometimes leads to dishonest and underhanded actions; as the addictive lure of being featured in the media; as invitations to awards ceremonies however specious they may be; as the tendency to make false personal and professional comparisons with industry peers; and sometimes as tedious boredom with professional life and the desire to retire early. The most important armour a founder can have against all such distractions is the discipline to say 'no'. What makes the difference is the individual's ability to choose what is right over what is convenient.

In my first book, *The High-Performance Entrepreneur,* I mentioned that most start-ups close down within the first year of their existence not due to adverse circumstances but because their founders part ways. It could be easily concluded from this that it is a great thing for an organization if its founders stay together for the long haul and grow with the company. Well, not really.

When an organization begins its operations, people work very closely with each other for the larger cause. The bond that develops between them is so strong and so alluring that people come to work responding to its call. As the organization gradually expands, the bond extends to the larger team. There it translates into dealing with adversities and solving crucial problems together. Individuals and teams fall back on each other and cover for each other, as if they are fighting in the trenches. As the company grows larger still and newer people join, the seemingly positive qualities of loyalty, the ability to complement each other, and ease of communication that the initial group shares, may begin to manifest itself as an altogether unanticipated, silently destructive behaviour: favouritism. It begins, like many other organizational malfunctions, in a benign manner.

Imagine a difficult, much-needed deal that requires careful, expert handling. What are the chances that a rank newcomer will be called to action? Or, for that matter, a project team constituting mostly new people runs into a terrible customer situation and the matter gets escalated. Who is called to perform damage control? It is, without doubt, the old guard.

As more instances of this recur, the rest of the employees in the organization get alienated and what could have developed as healthy rivalries, which can benefit the company in many ways, takes the unfortunate form of groupism, which can be destructive in the extreme.

Whenever there are multiple founders behind the setting up of a company, and they all choose to stay on, the inevitable issue of succession comes up. Key jobs go to the founders as a default. The formation of an inner circle is likely and, even if one doesn't exist, people assume it does. A few years back we were looking at candidates for a senior position at Mindtree. This was a critical role because we were at a turning point, mulling over the rebranding of the company. KK, Mindtree's CEO at the time, tapped into his network and zeroed in on a candidate in his early forties. He managed the marketing function of a larger entity and there was no doubt in our minds that Mindtree would be a great platform for him. We were relatively sure that he would accept our offer. But when KK reached out to him, he told KK that he wasn't keen. However attractive the job and the pay, he explained, he knew where he wanted to be in terms of his career and did not see himself becoming Mindtree's CEO within the next decade. KK was 52 at the time. After him there would be someone else and then someone else – the proverbial founders' queue, as it were. If he waited, he said, he would probably be ready to hang up his boots by the time his turn arrived. KK and I should have thought about this. It occurred to us at that point that there could be many others out there who felt the same way and had closed their minds to joining Mindtree because of it.

This brings us to the difficulty many founders have in letting go and the temptation they feel to overstay their welcome. Just as it is critical for founders to know when to start a company, it is equally critical for them to know when to leave it. This might be very difficult emotionally, particularly when a company might have fresh ambitions and a breakthrough moment may be at hand. But it is exactly at such a time that a founder should ask the question and answer it as objectively as possible: Will the company and its people be significantly better off in other hands? There is another aspect to this. A founder may feel that the organization is his house. After all, he built it. The truth is, he is *almost* right, not entirely so. Many people – customers, employees, investors and sometimes completely unrelated individuals – have helped at points of inflection and built on the foundation he laid.

For most, the timing of their exit is determined by financial opportunism and not a self-assessment of how much of the runway is still ahead. In today's world both expert guidance and examples of well-chosen exits are available for reference, but the process of wise detachment must begin in the mind of the founder and no one else.

As Khalil Gibran poignantly wrote:

'Your children are not your children...
They come through you but not from you,
And though they are with you they belong not to you.'

If that is hard to accept, just as hard is the truth that the enterprise is not the child of the entrepreneur; it has merely flown through him.

PART VI

SCALING AGAINST ADVERSITY

21

RITES OF PASSAGE

> "Despite good intent, a certain amount of failure, anguish, alienation and disappointment are rites of passage for every growing organization. If self-doubt takes over, it is wise to remember that pain is inevitable but suffering is optional."

IT IS RATHER UNUSUAL for a team of co-founders in any start-up to remain together for over a decade. At the time of writing this book, fourteen years into Mindtree, seven of us are still a part of the organization. What are the factors that have contributed to this unusual cohesion? It is a complex question, but the answers that immediately come to mind out are: a shared vision, common values and mutual trust. These have prevailed over the day-to-day grind of raising a company from the start-up level to public listing, and now beyond that. But this chapter is not about how we managed that process; it is about a few things that had escaped me until one of the ten co-founders left us.

A close-knit group of people completely overlooks that every individual in a group evolves over a period of time. Profound changes occur in everyone's lives. These are bound to impact an individual's outlook on life and work. When people work together for relatively shorter periods of time, say two or three years, this does not matter as much, but when a group has been together for ten years (and sometimes even five), such changes affect not only its members but also the organization as a whole. Some may be for the good, others not so much. Often, because the group works so closely, these changes remain unnoticed for a relatively long time. When they eventually surface, they may take the other members by surprise and lead to difficulties and complications in work relationships. A person who was once approachable may become reticent and not share as much as he did in the beginning. A person who only thought of work and led by example may appear to have given up and become lazy. The happy-go-lucky executive may suddenly become overly critical of others, and seem serious and irritable. I could go on and on. Accepting such changes in others, and having to acknowledge them in oneself, is never easy.

Let us look at the enormity of the changes that the founding group at Mindtree went through. Between 1999 and 2014, there were four weddings and two divorces, and some serious medical issues, in the lives of seven out of the ten founders and their immediate families. Nine babies were born, eleven of our children became teenagers, and eight of them crossed over to their twenties. Five members of the families of the founders passed away and, on a happier note, one grandchild arrived. Each of these was a life-changing event and each such event had a lasting impact on us, individually and ultimately as a group. And what about the group of leaders beyond the founders? In Mindtree, the number of senior people who have stayed together over fourteen years runs into hundreds. The enormity of the effect every individual's personal changes could have on the collective is indeed staggering. The journey of an organization actually hides countless individual journeys and its course is almost always determined by them.

There is no magic formula for managing the ups and downs that inevitably mark an organization's progress, for maintaining a state of harmony and sustaining levels of performance and productivity in trying times. But it helps to know that big changes, when they come, need to be understood in the context of the individuals involved. When you notice any of these changes for the first time in your organization, tell yourself it is not an aberration but a rite of passage. That in itself will significantly change your ability to accept the inevitable, positively influence your approach to issues and individuals, and help in subsequently dealing with them in a manner that balances personal needs and organizational imperatives.

Imagine you have started a company with a bunch of friends who are professionally at the top of their game, hardworking and emotionally invested. One takes charge of R&D, the other – a star salesperson – takes on rainmaking, the finance whiz takes charge of his area of expertise, and everyone does an outstanding job. Then ten years go by and suddenly you find the company stalling despite the same people being at the helm. The interim years have naturally brought on an increase in volume and complexity in particular areas of work, and now the person who was an exemplary performer looks like he's in difficulty. Here is what is happening: the person was a star ten years back. He is no longer one because the sky itself has changed. Some people scale; many do not. There are those who can manage it with some help, and many are even able to transform themselves to keep up with the demands of a growing organization, but most struggle. Worse, they fail. The natural response of the person's peers to such situations are disappointment and frustration, and sometimes anger, and there arises a general disharmony in work relationships.

As the organization enters a mature phase and scales its operations, employees working alongside the top management who have proved to be traditionally competent and loyal automatically become the choices for filling up newer roles that may emerge. A technical guy may get into a business development role while an administration guy may be put in charge of procurement or supply chain management. The management may have the best intentions for the employees while bringing about these changes, but they have probably underestimated how rapidly many functions in a growing organization can become complex and now require experts to handle them. The old crew will no longer be effective in performing these functions. Not only will the individual struggle with the role, but he may also pull the functions down to match his performance limitations. The situation may be further exacerbated if the management gives the person a long rope and waits to see how things progress.

From here, further complications may arise for both the individual and the organization. A person who has so far been successful but is now struggling in a new role will look to the organization to solve his problem, perhaps even help him with an alternative career path. As hard as the management may try, it is impossible for any organization to remove arterial clogs in every senior person's career. This results in disappointment and bitterness, and such negativity has a tendency to spread well beyond the individual. The option open to the management at this stage is to accept that the future requires greater realism and provide a customized retirement plan designed to honour the employee's past contributions. When a tree does not give any more fruit, a gardener must clear the space and plant anew; a farmer must know when to put a horse to pasture.

When a company begins its operations its engine room is alive and bustling. Pioneers sign up, there is a tremendous amount of camaraderie, of give and take. This environment seldom makes for a highly differentiated compensation-and-benefits philosophy. As the company begins to grow and make money, a clamour against what may seem like a socialistic approach to compensation and benefits slowly begins to surface. 'We simply do not distinguish the best from the average,' becomes the refrain. The leadership acknowledges the anomaly and a compensation-and-benefits specialist is brought in to initiate salary benchmarks with peers in the industry. A compensation-and-benefits philosophy is drawn up and announced. Then comes the acid test of the competence and performance assessment that everyone must go through to determine where they fit in the new scheme of things. Complications are bound to kick in once some of the proponents of the so-called highly differentiated compensation structure are told that they fall in the average category. These people feel progressively alienated, and fail to cross the chasm. The management that has now taken steps to lead the organization to the next level cannot get frustrated with every such case. At this turning point in the organization's growth trajectory you cannot expect everyone to make it to the next level.

Now we have to address a very difficult part. It concerns the age-old adage 'Familiarity breeds contempt'. In the first few years of operating, there is very little gap between the people at the helm of affairs and the next level. This is consistent with the warm and inclusive culture that is a requirement at that stage. There is a lot of back-patting and tomfoolery. As an organization grows rapidly, people often forget the need for decorum that must come with expansion because the leadership is now more visible both within the company and outside it. It is one thing to be open and informal and collegial; it is another to appear unprofessional. In addition, overt familiarity can come in the way of giving and taking tough feedback and placing performance ahead of friendship. It is not as if the old-world familiarity has to go away, but more that protocol must be respected in public because in the right place and in the right dose both have their purpose.

Despite good intent, top management openness, support for an individual's career development and the overall growth momentum of the organization, not everything will work out the way you want. Don't get disheartened; a certain amount of failure, anguish, alienation and disappointment are rites of passage that every growing company must encounter. These should not leave the leadership flustered or endlessly self-critical. If the existential question looms large and self-doubt takes over, remind yourself of the larger purpose and tell yourself that pain is inevitable but suffering is optional.

22

BOLTS FROM THE BLUE

> ❛ When extraordinary events overtake us, it is time to do ordinary things extraordinarily well. ❜

WHEN 9/11 STRUCK, MINDTREE was a fledgling company. We had a few customers and were less than 500 people in size. It wasn't easy dealing with the aftermath, from the point of view of both internal motivation and external opportunity. Internally, people were so shaken that they questioned the very existence of small companies like ours. Externally, new software development and deployment came to a halt because companies froze all discretionary expenses. Customers pulled back IT budgets and spent money only on maintaining existing applications that would help them keep the lights on. Application Maintenance was not our competence at the time, and in any case most such deals had already been locked in through multi-year contracts. Mindtree was a development shop. Our entire revenue came from developing new applications, not maintaining existing large applications. The saving grace in this depressing scenario was the second round of funding of $12 million that we had received. We knew that it had to be stretched for as long as possible. The fact is we survived that bleak time while many other IT services companies born around the same time as us, and sometimes better funded, simply vanished. Was it because we were brilliant? Did we have an extraordinary, innovative, breakthrough strategy that saw us through?

One of the things I have done diligently over the last decade and a half is to archive every single notebook I have used since Mindtree started. In exploring the answer to the two questions above, I thought I should go back and look at my notes from that time: What was engaging me? Who was I meeting? What points had I scribbled and what was I doodling?

Before I tell you my conclusions about how we got through that time, let me describe for you the overall situation after 9/11.

At that time we had three major customers: Avis and Franklin Templeton in the US, and Hindustan Unilever in India. After 9/11, Avis experienced serious turbulence because the travel industry was badly hit and in December of that year, following a botched launch of their website, avis.com, turned serious heat on us for things mostly not attributable to us. Thanks to the greatness of Avis's leadership, facts were put on the table and considered. They retained us, and we continue to work for them even today. At Franklin Templeton, we were locked in with a difficult customer who wanted us to work 'like McKinsey', but paid ordinarily and was tyrannical in his behaviour though he believed that this was his way of showing affection. Unilever remained steadily with us even as our engagement remained limited to working with them in India.

My notes tell me about three major prospect meetings we had during the time. One was with General Motors (GM) in Detroit. After listening to my pitch the buyer I was meeting told me, 'You are so small that GM can chew you and spit you out before you know it.' The good-natured observation was a way of saying, 'Go punch someone your own size.'

Following this entry are records of a meeting I had with the Automobile Association of America. In contrast to my meeting with the buyer from GM, this was a brilliant meeting. The buyer here had heard about Mindtree. He thought we were an outstanding company and could play a significant role in their business. He could not wait to get started. I felt heady after hearing that; the meeting renewed my faith in god. However, soon after that meeting the man lost his job and that door closed.

On another page, I found the notes I had made during a meeting with a man named Rahul Samant who ran the programme office for four CIOs of the Bank of America. He was sympathetic but had just concluded a large, multi-year deal with three giant IT companies. Nothing would open up soon for yet another and, this time tiny, company like ours, he said.

While this was the general situation outside Mindtree, the sentiments within the organization weren't very different. Referring to a conversation with the project teams, Kamran Ozair, a co-founder, told me, 'Faith in Mindtree is at an all-time low.' During a structured briefing, T.G.C. Prasad, then head of HR at Mindtree, pretty much echoed the sentiment when he put forward three things: that our employees in Bengaluru believed the company's growth was in question; that they would most probably miss out on the bonus component of their salary because it was linked to company-level parameters; and that hope all around was at its lowest.

After this I came across my talking points for an upcoming All Minds Meet, which is what we call townhall meetings in Mindtree. We had done business worth $16.2 million the year before and were looking at taking it to $19.5 million in 2002. The expected loss was $1.5 million on that revenue number. I compared that to where we were in 2012. We had a business of $440 million, we had gone public, we employed 11,000 people and worked with an impressive list of global customers. A far cry from the gloom and doom of 2002. To get to the bottom of what we did right to get out of the abyss, I looked at my to-do lists from that time.

One such was drawn exactly a year from 9/11. It was in preparation of an impending visit to India because at that time I was operating out of the US. Here is the list, as it has been scribbled in my handwriting by a much younger me.

India Trip Objectives

1. Mid-year review with head of People Function
2. Web update
3. Run 2 sessions on Customer Interactions Skills for engineers
4. Do a session on Quality
5. Meet Ms S of potential PR partner
6. Hire marketing manager
7. Pay plumbing contractor who repaired Missionaries of Charity building
8. Review disaster management with MoRE committee
9. Address All Minds Meet
10. Small group leaders' meeting at Mindset Conference Room
11. Deposit salary certificate in bank
12. Run 4 sessions for young managers on writing performance appraisal
13. Over weekends, do team outing with Project Managers

As you will see, nothing of what I have archived for the period following 9/11 says that we did something spectacular, something breathtakingly brilliant. Clearly, that was not the reason we survived.

When a Category 5 hurricane hits you, what do you do? It is time to focus on doing all the things under your control with more effort than you've ever put in. The 13 items I had listed were under my control. The outcome of the war on terror, and predictions on whether the recession would take a double-dip, were not.

It is true that at Mindtree we had had the foresight to be frugal even before 9/11 happened. We built a culture that respected investor money. It was not meant to be blown; it was meant to be grown. Prior to 9/11 Mindtree was not paying the top executives fancy salaries, no one was flying business-class, nor were we staying in expensive hotels. So we did not have to downgrade such costs. The additional measures we put in place as exigency did not convey sudden frugality. We had always been a transparent company but during the time of crisis we increased our transparency and communicated even more with our leadership teams, our investors and suppliers. We used the slack periods to train our people. The top management worked constantly in the trenches. They made cold calls and sat in on delivery meetings. They visited trade and financial analysts and met customers who did not have additional business to give us. We also sought help from the outside world to keep internal cohesion intact. I remember going to a bunch of professors at New York University and inviting them to facilitate sessions with senior managers on their way forward.

When extraordinary events overtake us, it is time to do ordinary things extraordinarily well. However, in situations like this most top-management leaders feel helpless because when people are afraid they ask questions to which no one has answers. Yet, leaders feel compelled to answer everything. They feel awkward to say, 'I have no idea, I really don't have an answer.' After all, for so long it was their business to have smart answers to every problem. Sometimes, when the answer is beyond the leader's realm, he must look elsewhere to find it. This became clear to us when our investor V.G. Siddhartha brought along a senior official from Nomura Securities to the Mindtree office in 2009. The official wanted to know what would happen to the IT services industry now that the world was in shambles. I really did not have an answer. Instead, I drew his attention to Siddhartha's family business.

Siddhartha's family has been cultivating coffee for many generations. Coffee is a cyclical crop. In some years it grows well, in some years it does not. Even in a good year an Indian farmer may have to face an adverse situation because Ethiopian or Brazilian farmers have had a bumper crop, causing a glut in the market and prices to slump below the cost of growing the crop. So what does the farmer do, I asked the man. Dump his plantations and join e-business? The farmer simply waits for the next season and, meanwhile, tends to his plants. Mindtree, I explained to him, was like our piece of land and we would treat it like the coffee-grower treats his plantations. We would not give up in despair; we would just have to be patient and wait for things to turn around.

Around the same time that I met this gentleman a group of Mindtree leaders were huddled around a table in our office. They were gloomy and anxious. One of them cited the fact that big competitors were floundering. Smarter companies were unsure, everyone was laying off people, closing offices, instituting pay cuts. In other words, elephants were drowning. And we were just sheep. He asked me what my take was on the situation.

I asked the group to imagine a typical Indian vegetable market. As you approach the vegetable market, you are first greeted by the really small sellers who squat on the ground mostly in the open air. They sell low-value stuff like ginger, lime, coriander leaves and green chillies, and so on. They do not use weighing scales; instead, they sell in small lots. Usually customers pay them in coins and small currency, and the seller puts the cash under the sack that doubles up as his seat. This man does not have an electric bulb lighting up his offerings. He uses a lantern.

As you go further into the market, you meet a different kind of trader. This person sells produce of higher value, like potatoes and onions and cabbages. He has a small cash box and, sometimes, an assistant. He has a proper weighing scale with weights. He gladly accepts a hundred-rupee note from a customer and his assistant runs out to get change from the neighbouring stall. He does not have permanent lighting, but a make-shift electricity connection lights up a bulb overhead.

Further inside you see the 'real' vegetable-seller, the big guy. He has a permanently erected platform, a digital weighing scale, and an extensive range of shiny produce. Ask for it and you will get it. In season or not, local produce or imported, he has it all. He has three assistants because from his high perch it is not easy to get down to where the vegetables are neatly arranged. While he oversees the larger picture, the three assistants are the salesmen. Next to the owner is a television and he watches soap operas when business is slow.

When a global crisis is making the headlines, when a Gartner, Forrester or Moody is telling you that the end is near, it is a good idea to first ask yourself which of the three vegetable-sellers you resemble most closely. If you are the ginger-seller you don't need to worry at all. If you are the intermediate guy you need to worry only if the local transport companies go on strike. Moody downgrading the Sovereign rating will not affect you in the least. If you are the platform guy with the television, only then will you need to worry about world trade and tariffs, and get anxious if a big ship carrying the high-value, high-margin broccolis and ice-berg lettuce imported from across the world has not berthed.

■

Notes from another day.

The difficult period following 9/11 eventually ameliorated. The world returned to what people termed as 'new normal'. Over the next several years, all the way until 2006, we worked hard to make up for lost time. We grew both in terms of sales and profitability. In 2007, we started planning for listing Mindtree at the stock exchanges. At this time I had a meeting with a senior person who wanted to leave Mindtree. I was trying to keep him back.

He was 38, and a brilliant individual by any reckoning. In matters of finance, you just could not argue with him; among his peers, he was the acknowledged stock-market guru. In his first job with CRISIL he had evaluated companies. There he was viewed as an expert in figuring out which company had a strategy and which was a straggler. Then he worked at Grindlay's before moving to TCS. TCS sent him to Switzerland, where his client was the financial giant UBS. After TCS, he came via Infosys to Mindtree where he was seen as a star, albeit a restless one.

At that moment, seated in my office, he was being clairvoyant about two things: his own future and that of Mindtree. First, his own future. He wanted to retire by the time he was 48 and that was a good ten years away, but to do that he had to make money quite quickly. He did not see Mindtree taking him there, he declared. This brought him to his predictions about the company. His verdict was clear. He knew companies like Mindtree would run out of steam and never go public. The stock options given to employees like him weren't going to be worth the paper they were written on. He could prove it to me through a well-honed statistical model that he had developed, he said. I tried in vain to hold him back, but on that rather ominous note he quit.

Listening to him, my mind went back to when I had been 24. Many people do not know that I did a six-month stint in HCL at the time. It took just that much time for me to know that I would not be culturally compatible with the organization. This should not be construed as HCL being problematic in any way. Quite the other way around. After all, not everyone is meant for everyone else. So I left HCL, and as I was leaving and for a long time thereafter I was convinced that the company would go nowhere in the future. I was dead wrong on that count, and looking back I realize it was not only an absurd view but also an unwarranted one. Two decades later, HCL is a well-known company with a multi-billion-dollar sales turnover, many loyal customers and happy employees. My perception of it was exactly that – *my perception.*

So, what do my notes taken in good times and bad really tell me? Building and leading an organization that will scale one day isn't everyone's cup of tea. For it to reach this stage, before everything else, it must survive. If you look for evidence in your immediate environment you'll see that survival is difficult. Life requires that you hang in there even if it defies reason and seems foolish. Survival is predominantly a state of mind.

While flipping through my notes, I also came across a list of my talking points for a leadership off-site. The list startled me. It did not look like something from a decade-old notebook. The issues I had flagged appeared relevant even in the present. As you go through them, you will notice that they are universal and timeless, and could well be about *your* company, in the year 2020.

- Are we communicating enough, communicating well and communicating with confidence?
- Are we fixing issues at the point of occurrence?
- Are we abdicating roles?
- Are we transmitting
    - Being overwhelmed?
    - Burnt out?
    - Personal insecurity?
    - Uncertainty about the future?

- Are we more customer-facing and less constituent (our own people)-facing?
- How do we practice inclusion?
  - How many people are involved in decision-making?
  - Do we have weekly debriefs?
  - Do people interact outside work at a personal level?
- How are we breaking down the CTP [a company from which a few founders and some senior people had come] issue? Is there a firm way to put it to rest?
- Are we cohesive enough?

There is just one conclusion to draw from this. Whatever the circumstance, an organization's leaders cannot get overwhelmed. In any given circumstance both irrational exuberance and doomsday prophecies have an uncanny knack for going wrong. Leaders have to recognize issues as they are, and deal with them as best they can. In doing so, they must listen to the voices of dissent (there is often wisdom and courage resting there) but should not get discouraged by the prophets of doom. And, finally, they must preserve faith in order to build an organization that will outlive them.

ACKNOWLEDGEMENTS

The Elephant Catchers would not have come to life but for the support of my publisher, Thomas Abraham, whom I have known for many years. He believed in the need for a book like this one, and I deeply value his constant encouragement over the years of our association.

My editor, Poulomi Chatterjee, has been extremely patient with the many early drafts. When I revisited them from time to time, I marvelled at her kindness. She must have been my kindergarten teacher in our last life.

I am indebted to Dr Partha Mukhopadhyay at the Centre for Policy Research; Tridip Saha, a colleague at Mindtree; Sambuddha Deb, with whom I have worked for many years prior to Mindtree; and my daughter Neha for going through the first-cut of the book and pointing out the gaps that I later addressed.

Doris Abraham, a student of mass communication at the Manipal University, was my official fact-checker. I am grateful to her for her time and diligence.

I am indebted to my longtime reader Geetha Chandar who went through the manuscript and made several important suggestions during the early stages.

Without my writer wife Susmita's support I would be nowhere in my professional endeavours. She has never grudged my holed-in existence in my study weekend after weekend. With great happiness, or so I believe, she has kept my synapses irrigated with the best tea anyone can make in this world. The most reassuring thing in my parallel life as a writer of business books is the framed cross-stitch creation that hangs in our kitchen. It says, 'ANY TIME IS TEA TIME'.

AFTERWORD

NEW STORIES, FURTHER LESSONS

23

AMAZING STORIES OF SCALE

> 'Businesses do not simply achieve scale because they do their job amazingly well. That is a given. Invariably, businesses that scale become known for doing something significant outside of their business.'

AFTER *THE ELEPHANT CATCHERS* was published, at the invitation of the Confederation of Indian Industry (CII), I had the opportunity to travel to a dozen non-metro cities in the country to speak with emerging companies in India on the topic of scaling up. CII had a unique initiative called the 'Golden Top' programme to accelerate mid-size companies to double or treble their growth. It provided the organizations with key benchmark indicators to determine their progress and achievement, helped them create a network for opportunities and, of course, granted rewards and recognition for every milestone achieved, thus encouraging them to strive for more. The idea behind the initiative was the realization that there is no dearth of entrepreneurship in the country, but there is scarcity of scale.

The assignment took me to places across the country – Jaipur, Lucknow, Chandigarh, Ahmedabad, Pune, Vizag, Coimbatore, Kochi and many others – and some of the stories I heard, of local companies scaling up in innovative, unexpected ways, left me spellbound; I saw in them bold traces of the ideas I have tried to put forward in this book. At the same time, there were new learnings, especially on the challenges of scaling up, and why companies across the country fail to do so quickly and effectively. In this afterword, I present to you some of these stories and the different facets of scale they represent.

Scaling Your Vision

Chances are, unless you are from Kerala, you haven't heard of Beena Kannan. She is the force and spirit behind a saree business that goes by the name of Seematti and lives by its tagline 'The Queen of Silks'. Beena was born into a family that owned a few saree shops in places like Kottayam and Kochi. The only child of her parents, Beena was married early to her childhood friend, Kannan, who joined the family business and, effectively, took charge of it. Tragically, he died of cancer within the next few years. By now the mother of three toddlers, Beena had no option but to step up and take over her late husband's reponsibilities, three days after her husband passed away.

At the time Beena took over the reins of the business, the saree as an attire was increasingly losing out to other forms of clothing that were perceived to be more manageable and contemporary. Weaving communities across the country, custodians of ageless artisanship, were losing out to mill-made, cost-effective synthetic sarees. Amidst this spectre, Beena did something seemingly counter-intuitive. She put all her might behind traditional weaves. She contemporized traditional designs after conducting intense research into weaving techniques and the history of the garment itself, and by working closely with weavers.

At the same time, Beena began to present and redefine the saree as a garment that was youthful, sensuous, chic, and an object of desire through a brand campaign that made Seematti a household name in Kerala in the next few years. To know what I mean, go on to YouTube and watch the two iconic advertisements that showcase Seematti's products. One is shot on location in Europe and the other in Africa. The first weaves the story of an Indian girl whose sensuous charm attracts a young Dutch painter who follows her from one place in Europe to another until she responds favourably to his attentions at the base of the Eiffel Tower. The second shows a supermodel clad in Seematti's creations camping in the African wilderness. She charms African tribesmen and wild, ferocious animals, who follow in her steps, mesmerized by her beauty and grace. My descriptions of the two ad films do not do justice to their true worth. Yes, a lot of resources, especially money, have gone into the making of the films, but money alone does not buy the creative ideas behind the films or their spectacular execution. The films have been made only because Beena was able to envision her product and her business on a completely different level. The setting, the cast, the cost and everything else followed. Beena created spectacular, spellbinding advertising because she believed in scale.

Just as she redefined the product, Beena redefined the customers' buying experience as well. She travelled extensively, studied the best retail experiences provided by brands around the world and designed her outlets in a way that had not been done before in the saree business. Yet, even as her own business became greatly successful, Beena did not lose sight of the weaver communities. Always mindful that it was their art, their vision and their labour that went into the creation of the exquisite weaves she was presenting, she helped to expand their repertoire on the one hand while introducing their skills to larger groups of consumers on the other. Today these communities revere her for reviving what could clearly have been a dying business for them.

Beena Kannan is an exemplar of scale at many levels. If she had not been able to rise above her tragic circumstances,

Seematti would have probably gone down as an incidental loss. But Beena focused her energy on transforming a business that others would have seen simply as a holding-pattern idea rather than one with breakthrough possibilities. That focus, combined with spectacular creative thinking, strategic positioning of her product and relentless execution, made it possible for her to transform nine-yard stretches of a beautiful but somewhat binding textile into an aspirational item for buyers. Today, Beena has taken the saree to high-profile catwalks, wrapped them around supermodels and showcased them as haute couture. In Kerala, Seematti's sarees are an essential item at weddings, and its annual bridal collections are, in fact, anticipated and awaited across the state.

In every Indian town and city, there might be two, or maybe three, saree shops that everyone knows about. They have probably existed as long as Seematti has, but they haven't scaled. They have remained local saree and garment businesses while Seematti, helmed by Beena Kannan, has reached new heights.

Scaling Up, and Around

Not many people, even those who track businessmen in India, would know Soundararajan Bangaruswamy and G.B. Sundararajan. The two men are siblings, born to school-teacher parents in Ganapathipalyam, a village located five kilometres away from Udmalpet town in Tamil Nadu. When elder brother Soundararajan finished school, his parents dissuaded him from going to college and asked him to make something of the small patch of land they owned. Young Soundararajan worked very hard but ran into difficulties and debt because his land's produce didn't have access to markets. Even today, this remains a huge problem for many Indian farmers. You may produce great vegetables but if they do not reach the mandi or the shelves of a supermarket in time, they will not find buyers. A time came when he was no longer able to pull the farm out of difficulties and was sent off by the family to Hyderabad to work as a shop hand. Soundararajan didn't know the local language. Unable to engage in verbal negotiation when a customer began to haggle, he would write his offer on a piece of paper. The customer would then write down a counter offer and, eventually, after considerable paper pushing, a deal would be struck.

While Soundararajan was away, Sundararajan, his younger sibling by two years, finished school, briefly went to college in a nearby town and returned to his village. There, he chanced upon a cousin raising broiler chicken to sell them and an idea struck him. Could this be the solution to all their financial difficulties, he wondered. Sundararajan returned home with a few newly hatched chicks from his cousin's clutch and called his brother back from Hyderabad. The two put their heart and soul into their newly established business and, this time, having learnt the consequences of poor market access, decided to set up shop in Udmalpet town itself so that they could retail the chicken where the buyers were. The two brothers located a shop owned by their father's friend and made a pitch to rent it. The owner was initially sceptical but finally let out the place to them.

The business, known today as Suguna Foods, took off. To raise the birds, the brothers bought chicken feed from a company in Mysore. Gradually, it occurred to them that they could also become resellers of chicken feed to their fellow farmers in and around their village. This is no small breakthrough in entrepreneurial thinking. I call it sensing the power of adjacency. Most entrepreneurs become so focused on their core business that they do not see the paths of profit that lie adjacent. The brothers executed a classic example of harvesting adjacency in exactly the same way as Starbucks. Starbucks's core product is coffee but it also sell products adjacent to coffee – such as sandwiches, water, coffee mugs and expensive coffee-making equipment for personal use.

This worked out well until a farmer complained to the chicken-feed manufacturer that the brothers were mixing spurious stuff in the bags shipped by the manufacturer, and the manufacturer sent in a quality inspector. The inspector arrived to verify the facts and though the allegations proved to be baseless, the brothers were offended and angered. Not only did they stop buying chicken feed from the manufacturer, but they also decided, almost immediately, to enter the chicken feed market themselves. From that point onwards, there was no looking back. Now they were raising chicken, and selling chicken and chicken feed as well. But the two brothers were still not satisfied and continued to think of ways to expand their business. It was then that they hit upon the idea of contract farming to take advantage of the abundance of space in the village and the leisure time the villagers had on their hands. The brothers asked local farmers to set up chicken coops on their unutilized land. They gave these farmers the chicks, the training to raise them, supplied feed and vaccines and, after 45 days, paid for the broilers and took them to market. This new venture brought them phenomenal success. Today, Suguna Foods does not raise a single bird. More than 23,000 farmers do that on their behalf. Their business is no longer contained within Tamil Nadu and has expanded in many Indian states and beyond, to Sri Lanka and Bangladesh. As of the fiscal year 2017, their business clocks revenues of more than ₹5,200 crores and employs 5,500 people.

Scaling Your Reputation

Revenue growth is not the only way to look at scale. A lot of it has to do with reputation-building. Take the case of Melam, a spice company based in Kerala. The company, started in 1992, built a recognized, differentiated spice brand at home and overseas, grew to 16 distribution centres, and was honoured for outstanding export performance. In 1997, Melam founder Kurian John Melamparambil was awarded the Padma Shri by the Government of India and, in 2015, the business and the brand was acquired by the AVA Group. Ask anyone in Kerala and they will tell you that Melam means quality, and they will also tell you about the company's outreach programme, by means of which, by 2013, Melam had served 12.5 million poor patients with critical needs in government hospitals.

The Melam example and countless such – big and small, national and global – tell me that businesses do not simply achieve scale because they do their job amazingly well. In today's world, you are expected to deliver excellence in what you do. That is a given. Invariably, businesses that scale become known for something significant they do outside of running their core business. It could be their approach to people, their engagement with local issues, charity work, their commitment to raising the standards of their suppliers, or their contribution to their industry for collective success beyond narrow competition.

In other words, companies that scale stand for something solid. This often stems from the personality of the leader at the top, the cause that deeply affects the leader and then permeates down to the culture of the organization. Take Ujjivan, one of India's most admired micro-finance companies, for instance. Not only does it do its job exceedingly well, it has been featured, year after year, in the prestigious Great Place to Work list, rubbing shoulders with giants like Google, SAP, Shell and others. Today, from a small micro-finance company, Ujjivan has become a bank. To founder Samit Ghosh, outstanding employee engagement, the core element of the Great Place to Work competition, is an idea that goes beyond business. Ujjivan doesn't just value its top line and bottom line, it wants to be famous for its people practices.

Ganga Hospital in Coimbatore is another such example. This family-led, 450-bed orthopaedic hospital is of international repute. Ganga Hospital performs 2,000 spine surgeries a year and has its own – and India's first hospital-owned – air-ambulance service. They fix bones and flesh and sinews all right, but alongside their daily practice the founders, Dr S. Raja Sabapathy and Dr S. Rajasekaran, relentlessly amplify the voice against medical and pharmaceutical malpractices to the level that you would mistake them for activists. At the same time, and with equal zeal, they continuously raise the conversation for policy and practice changes for road safety in India, a country where one fatal accident takes place every six minutes.

The need to build reputational capital beyond the soap or candy, the loan product or the surgical equipment you are manufacturing and selling is becoming critical in a world exploding with competitive choices in almost every field. Today, it is not enough to have a great product. To be labelled a successful business, you need to do something else exceptionally well.

24

THE CHALLENGES TO SCALING UP

> 'Sometimes, those who opt out of the choice to scale up say that they do not wish to take on any "unnecessary headache". Such thoughts arise from their underlying fear of the loss of quality and, hence, reputation that they have striven to build.'

WHILE I HAVE SEEN some spectacular examples of scaling up in every region of India and in every sector, I have encountered many more businesses that possess the potential to scale but are simply not able to. In my interactions with these companies, I have noticed a set of reasons that prevents them from breaking the proverbial ceiling.

Of these, the most recurring reason that seems to plague small- and medium-sized companies is filial love. It may sound surprising, but it is true. When organizations are owner-driven, the business's innate ability to scale becomes secondary to the choice of people whom the owner or founder can depend upon. Thus, sons and daughters – still usually in that order – who have invariably been groomed by a patriarch, become beholden to the need for cohesion and harmony within the family ahead of everything else. They hold on to the belief that everyone must defer to the head of the family and the values engendered in them over generations are the true crown jewels. Even as the third, and sometimes the fourth generation, comes into business, they find it difficult to move beyond the boundaries of the success that has been achieved so far. Most of these family-run businesses do not scale for another reason: they fail to attract outstanding external talent. This means that the family members themselves are considered to be the most competent people in the firm. These members – their bandwidth and their personal motivation – thus end up defining how far the organization will go.

Yet, there are family-run businesses that attract great talent. But this requires thinking very differently at a strategic level, creating structural arrangements, putting in place governance mechanisms and consistently defining the organization's culture.

Another common reason why family-run companies in India do not achieve scale is poor governance. Many well run and foundationally strong companies do not scale further because they are not transparent about their wealth and what they are doing with it. Under-reporting of wealth and legally untenable business practices force companies to keep too many secrets and the owners see themselves as protectors of these secrets. Scaling up is avoided because that could make their wealth visible and draw undue attention to their practices. It could also mean that more people would now have to be taken into confidence about the hidden aspects of the business. Thus, in some cases, even though there is great potential for a business to grow, its owners prefer to contain it.

Another interesting phenomenon that inhibits scale is the fear of displacement. This is often as basic as not wanting to leave the geographic confines of a town or a state. Take, for instance, the municipal town of Tiruppur in the southern state of Tamil Nadu, an hour's drive from Coimbatore. With a working population of approximately 6,00,000, the town has several small- and medium-sized companies – all of them in the business of manufacturing knitted garments for global brands and mostly owned by first- and second-generation businessmen. Although in Tiruppur a business turnover of ₹250 crore makes you 'big', in 2017 the town's collective revenue amounted to a spectacular ₹45,000 crore. Close to 70 per cent of this total revenue came from exports.

In 2014, the owners of the town's knitwear units, under the aegis of Tirupur Exporters Association (TEA), built a lofty goal to establish a ₹1 lakh-crore business by 2020, which meant more than doubling the turnover the companies under its governance have collectively clocked so far in 2017. This was – and remains – an ambitious plan by any reckoning, and the owners know they cannot achieve it from within Tiruppur. It is simply not the sort of goal that can be attained by linear growth and by continuing to do business as usual. They realize that a core element of the strategy they have to embrace is physical displacement and that they have to learn to replicate the Tiruppur model elsewhere by setting up manufacturing businesses and partnerships outside the township.

Yet, as strong as their resolve is to live up to their goal, they find it a daunting task. When you speak to them they love to tell you why the Tiruppur story is unique and cannot be replicated elsewhere. They talk about the one attempt that was made to set up manufacturing units as close as at Madurai, which failed for various reasons, and insist that the DNA of the township is so unique and the secret alchemy so specific to it that the model would not work outside Tiruppur. Their attitude is obviously contradictory to their ambition for growth. When you dig deeper, you can see their discomfort with – even their fear of – physical displacement.

The fear of physical displacement is not something that grips the companies of Tiruppur alone. In any other state, too, you will find successful businesses reluctant to go to other parts of the country for fear of the unknown. The state of domicile thus becomes a comfort zone and a consequent limit to growth for many enterprises.

A great counter-example of bucking the fear of physical displacement can be witnessed in the story of Wipro's Chairman, Azim Premji. Premji decided to move his corporate office from Mumbai and personally shifted to Bengaluru in the mid-1990s even though Wipro had started in Mumbai in 1947 and the Premjis had lived there for generations. Premji's move to Bengaluru accelerated the company's forays into Information Technology (IT) businesses and was the starting point from which the company has today grown to become one of the most respected IT services companies in the world.

Related to this is the fear of losing control and the fear of letting go. The fear of losing control is endemic to many proprietor–founders. This happens when the person at the helm believes that expanding into new kinds of businesses will entail hiring more professionals in key jobs and, sometimes, physical displacement. Both situations may bring about a sense of losing control. The proprietor–owner may feel that personal control is more important than customer centricity and innovation.

Yet, there are examples galore where business owners see control as a less important goal than wealth creation. Take the example of GMR, a company that was relatively unknown a decade ago. Today, you cannot ignore them when you pass through the Indira Gandhi International Airport in New Delhi. To GMR founder G.M. Rao, it is not control that is the obsession, it is scaling up. The story repeats itself in many other enterprises, including in the telecommunications company Airtel, which did not exist before 1995. Today it operates in 18 countries and has posted revenues of $15 billion in 2017 till date.

Another fear that retards scale is the fear of what I call 'the platform'. When people build companies and organizations, the platform, at first, is small, intimate, manageable. Once the company attains a certain size, the business becomes a living entity, so to speak, with a platform that is quite independent of its creators. It is as if a child, once a part of you, has suddenly become an adult. Now the founder/owner/creator must make critical choices, either to keep the organization at a particular size or aspire to breach it. The latter may mean many things: New kinds of employees, new products and services, new locations, new clients, and new collaborators, suppliers and franchisees.

Sometimes, those who opt out of the choice to scale say that they do not wish to take on any 'unnecessary headache'. Such thoughts arise from their underlying fear of loss of quality and, hence, the reputation that they have striven to build. Interestingly, entrepreneurs who have achieved scale do not fear the platform; they suffer least of all from the fear of loss of quality and reputation. Where others dread the oft-quoted 'dilution of standards', these people do not lose sleep over it. Instead, they invest in protecting themselves against such eventualities and thus treat as non-issues the factors that may appear to others as a huge risk.

It is valid to perceive risk in scaling. But to be held back by the thought of a temporary setback – that can never lead to scale.

Perhaps the most pervasive reason for not scaling up that I have seen in the companies I have interacted with is an inability to see ahead of the curve. Sometimes people at the top believe they know the reason for their organization not achieving scale when they simply do not have this knowledge. This is a common folly among high performers. People who create organizations, people who lead them, are categorized as 'Type A' personalities. Such people, by their own makeup, are ambitious, competitive, driven, opinionated and super-confident. These are virtues that engender obstinacy against odds and the tenacity to stay the course – qualities that have been put to good use in building their businesses thus far. Yet, after about a decade spent on growing the business, leaders might not be able to envision the more distant future. This is when they run out of ideas for growth or begin to lack the foresight to see that the larger business environment no longer favours their products and services. Change is inevitable.

Camera rolls give way to flash memory. E-tail overruns brick-and-mortar retail. Yellow-top cabs vanish and college students drive a hail-a-ride in their free time. Telcos becomes the new bank and smartphone companies go on to manufacture cars. Those who fail to decode these tectonic (or shall we say 'tech-tonic') shifts, who fail to look ahead and have the vision to scale their organizations in accordance to changing market environments, falling back instead on conventional intelligence or their own faith in the ability to 'know when the time is right', end up with a business that does not look to the future, one that is bound to become obsolete.

25

THE SIX ELEMENTS OF SCALING UP

> "The six elements of scale are like the six horses of a chariot. Organizations that achieve scale pay attention to the six horses in equal measure so that the three essentials of successful business - time, direction and speed - work to their profit."

Organizations that have scaled up, and not just in terms of their top line and bottom line, do six things rather well.

- They are strongly identified with a given domain.
- They develop unique methodology that helps them to do their job well and, more crucially, focus on building and perfecting the methodology that helps them to replicate their genes.
- They apply unrelenting focus on quality.
- They are constantly innovating in terms of product, process and service delivery.

- And last, but not the least, they understand the essence of branding.

One of the best examples of an organization that has managed to overcome enormous obstacles to build scale in India is Aravind Eye Hospital.

Started by Dr Govindappa Venkataswamy, better known as Dr V, Aravind Eye Hospital is the world's largest eye hospital in terms of the millions of patients they treat and operate upon.

In Part VI of this book, I have spoken about the ability to scale adversity as a key requirement of scaling. This often manifests at a personal level for the leader of an organization and the response of the individual may determine the outcome of the organization in a very substantial manner. Dr V is a great example of that. Raised in a tiny hamlet in Tamil Nadu, Dr V was deeply moved by the death of a young woman in his neighbourhood when he was a young boy. She had not survived complications developed during childbirth and had succumbed to the physical trauma brought about by her condition. He decided right then that he would study to become a doctor. He pursued his goal, studied medicine and joined the Army. Within a year of beginning his career as a physician, he was struck by a rare form of rheumatoid arthritis that crippled him and left him with crooked fingers and toes. Since he was no longer able to do his job, the Army discharged him. Not daunted by this massive setback, the young doctor rebuilt his life, this time qualifying himself as an ophthalmologist, and trained his crooked fingers to hold surgical instruments with such great precision that he went on to perform more than 100,000 intricate eye surgeries in his lifetime. At 58, he retired from his job as an eye surgeon with the state government of Tamil Nadu and set up Aravind Eye Hospital. The story of Dr V's determined journey towards his vision, led by his singular sense of purpose, has become undeniably and deeply embedded in the meta-consciousness of the organization he founded. When such purpose is the foundation on which an organization is built, it engenders resilience in every function within the organization, giving it the necessary character and tools to deal with the setbacks that would otherwise come in the way of scaling up. In the four decades of its existence, Aravind Eye Hospital has seen more than 50 million patients, conducted more than 6 million operations and, amazingly, with the money it receives from 30 per cent of its patients – the 'paying patients' – today provides free medical services to the 70 per cent who cannot pay.

If you take the hospital and its founder as case studies in building scale, you'll see that they tick all the boxes. ***Not only have they strongly identified themselves in their domain – ophthalmology – but they are also masters of methodology.*** They recognized right at the outset that their ability to treat patients from a single, central location would limit the number of patients they would be able to treat. Early entrants in the game of telemedicine, they set up village-based vision centres managed by one or two trained nurses who could perform routine optometry locally. Armed with a digital camera and a low-bandwidth connection to their base hospital, these emergency medical personnel have been enabled to upload pictures, video-confer with doctors in real time and download prescriptions. When the circumstance necessitates it, they can arrange to send patients to the base hospital for surgery. The idea of assembly-line operations in hospitals also started here. Conventionally, surgeons move from one operation theatre to another to perform procedures on different patients. Aravind created its own methodology. At Aravind Eye Hospital, it is not the surgeon who physically moves from one location to the other but the patients, already prepped for surgery, who are brought to them. This simple method sharply increases each doctor's productivity while ensuring that patients get treatment and relief sooner rather than later.

This does not mean that the hospital loses focus on quality in any way. In fact, ***their commitment to providing the best medical attention is legendary.*** They achieve this by means of putting their core philosophy into practice: Placing the 'customer', in this case a patient, paying or non-paying, at the centre of their existence. They focus on the stated and unstated needs of the 'customer' in ways that many Six Sigma companies would consider the benchmark.

Consider this: the incidence of premature babies is very high in villages where girls who are married off early get pregnant and maternal malnutrition is pervasive. A pre-term baby is often at a high risk of a particular vision problem that requires a simple laser procedure that can save the child from blindness. However, such a condition must be diagnosed within the first few weeks. The problem is that the baby cannot report its discomfort, and the mothers and the healthcare system too are not equipped to check and report such an incidence. This is where Aravind steps in. The hospital dispatches a couple of trained nurses in a van mounted with a sophisticated diagnostic machine. This team goes from one birthing centre to the next to check and bring back a mother and her child to a base hospital if a surgical procedure is necessary. This practice is a great example of expanding the essence of quality by literally going the extra mile to explore the unstated needs of the customer.

Talk about innovation and, once again, Aravind scores high. The hospital uses information technology tools to the hilt. The receptionist of their out-patient department has been equipped with a predictive chart of footfall on any given day. She knows when there will be a surge of patients and can accordingly advise you on the date and time of your appointment. The predictive model takes into account the last few decades of data for a given day of the week, the lunar calendar (no one in southern India will schedule a surgery during a new moon phase), the school holiday list for the year, and so on. If schools are closed on a Monday, there will be a surge of patients; if school examinations are about to begin parents will not be bringing their children to the hospital for an eye examination.

The innovation doesn't stop there. Dr V realized soon after establishing the hospital that intraocular lenses, that is, the lenses that are implanted in the eye after a cataract is removed, are expensive and unaffordable for poor patients – each lens costing upwards of $100. Through collaborations with international organizations, he started manufacturing the lenses locally and was able to drive that price of the lenses to less than $5 per piece. To manufacture these lenses, Dr V recruited girls who were high-school graduates from villages and trained them to run sophisticated precision equipment and robotic systems. Not only did the affordability of the lenses create a revolution in eye care in the country, but the infrastructure set up for their manufacture provides employment opportunities and income to inhabitants, particularly girls, in a number of villages.

Finally, Aravind Eye Hospital is an ace in branding. But when I say branding in relation to them I do not mean high-budget marketing campaigns and the use of social media, which have now become synonymous with the word. The true meaning of branding is the act of externalizing the inner worth of an organization. Aravind does that remarkably well by making its methodology and functional solutions available to organizations around the world. The number of external doctors and nurses who have been trained at the hospital is legion.

Dr V and the Aravind Eye Hospital have raised the bar on achieving scale in every possible way. It is no wonder that theirs is a case study taught at Harvard Business School and top executives routinely visit the hospital to learn management practices they can take back to apply in their for-profit businesses.

The six elements of scale: domain, tools, methodology, quality, innovation and branding, are like the six horses of a chariot. Many organizations know that. But the ones that scale pay attention to the six horses in equal measure so that the three essentials of successful business – time, direction and speed – work to their profit. Simply put, the six horses must pull the chariot at the same time, in the same direction and at the same speed. That is the essence of scaling up.

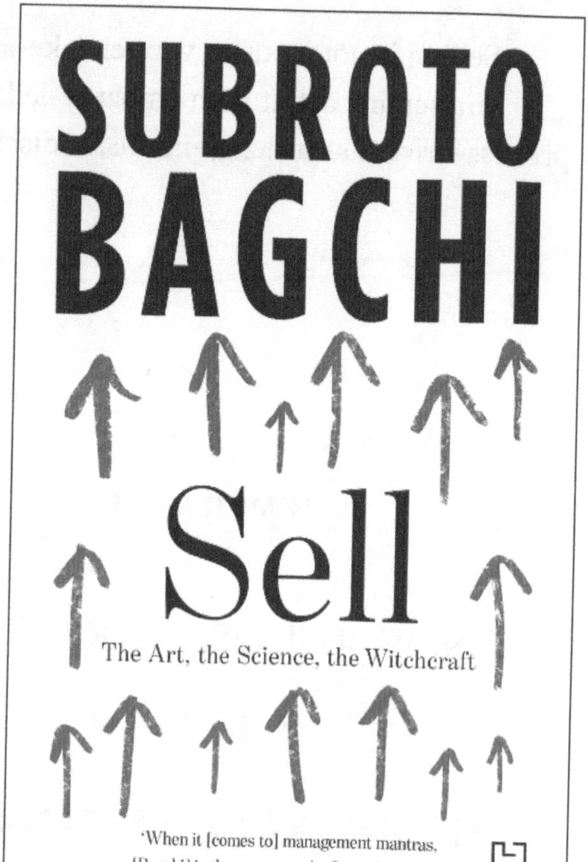

ISBN 9789350095829 | ₹499

ABOUT THE BOOK

An inspiration to a generation of entrepreneurs, Subroto Bagchi considers himself a career salesman, of products, services and ideas.

In his new book, *Sell*, Bagchi presents the concepts of selling and salesmanship from his unique perspective. Through stories and anecdotes drawn from his repertoire of experiences, extensive reading and the careers of ace professionals he has encountered in his life, Bagchi touches on each stage of the traditional selling process and elaborates on the skills, tools and nuances that he believes can take the profession to the realm of art – and sometimes even wizardry.

Dip into this book to get insights into:

- How knowing about the life-cycle of the coho salmon will help you prospect better;
- Distinguishing real customers with purchasing power from time-wasters who will merely give you the runaround;
- How creating a playbook well in advance can guarantee you a sale;
- The transformational effect of believing in the value of your product and how you can bring your customer around to share your vision;
- Why the power of persuasion ranks higher than the power to convince, and why persistence tends to become meaningless after a point.

Marked by Bagchi's characteristic wisdom and practicality, Sell is a rich, illuminating and contemporary treatise on salesmanship that dispels a narrow view of the act of selling and redefines it as a skill every professional needs to succeed in their career.